water soup

winter

two thousand
and fifteen

I0532702

ISBN: **0692646191**
ISBN-13: 978-0692646199

WaterSoup.Org

Contents

Los Angeles
Martha Martinez

As I sit on this dusty chair,looking at the green brown leaves, I wonder, exactly during what time do they start changing colors?

Then I remembered I was in Los Angeles.

I stop and start wondering again,

This time, I wonder as the driver drives down the noisy streets.

Next stop, Alvarado Street.

Looking at the diverse of people walking around and wonder,

"Are they wondering too?"

They are all in their own world,

you can see it through their blank faces.

The bus takes off, so I start walking.

The street is semi quiet it's 8:00am.

The smell of cigars and dumpster

stops me from keep on wondering.

It's ok, it's time for me to get to work.

I'll just keep wondering tomorrow.
It's enough for today.

3

Headline
Madison Lawson

I trusted him.

It's my loudest thought.

But its volume in my head is a dull whisper

Compared to what is thrashing and screaming in my dad's head.

One morning it's

Good morning. Thanks for the coffee. How are the kids?

One day it's

My dad, senior pastor, standing at the front,

Welcoming the members of staff,

Him sitting across the table from my dad,

Smiling, ideas ready to be shared for the good of the church.

Assistant pastor, trusted by my dad.

The others oblivious to the demons controlling his every movement.

Today my father wakes up to

Hundreds of messages, insults, accusations, comments laced with disgust

A sea of hidden faces, screaming into a void hoping to be heard,

Not aware of the impact their written words carry.

All: You knew. You protected and helped him. You're a fake. A predator too.

No: I'm sorry your close, trusted friend and employee did this.

No: I'm sure this is stressful and hard on you.

Just abuses hidden behind computer screens.

I sit, back against the wall,

Eyes consumed in tears, chest hot with shock.

I focus on the few messages directed at me

Daughter of senior pastor,

probably also aware of his staff member's extra-curricular activities.

I trusted him.

Public unaware of the pain spreading through my family..

In a roar ignited by a news story headline.

ASSISTANT PASTOR TRIED FOR SEXUALLY ABUSING YOUNG BOYS

Involuntary Aubade
Madison Lawson

A current of crisp aroma drifts through

Windows shoved up

Curtains haphazardly whipping

Free flow of morning breeze

Nose crinkling, I lay facedown.

Golden swords of light pierce my eyes

My skin itches with warmth.

Toes stretch out, searching

With much struggle, lids pull wide

Before slamming shut once more.

The dawn playlist shuffles

Glorious screeching of winged rodents

Striking whispers of evening promises

The current's song pushing against leaves

No one presses pause, it never stops.

He lays unmoving, chest lifting and falling

I drag my finger

Against his arm, painting.

The dawn pushes against my chest

And the curve of his lashes remind me

I'm not meant to be here.

I didn't want to be here.

My ultimate aid to life
Madison Lawson

When the morning sun pulls at me,

while I let night's sheet billow over my body,

as I sit in front of the keyboard and

silence purrs in the corners of my mind,

tickling my fingertips as

friends drag on dulled out conversations,

I'll have it steaming in my hands.

It's a simple thing, really.

No one thinks of it and says,

"Yes, it's what makes me smile, too."

But it does, for me, it paws at all my emotions.

It's a part of my life's steady rhythm.

A moment in each ordinary day.

A piece to my habitual puzzle.

It provides a comfort, the subtle perfection.

So when the morning sun pulls at me

the first thing I do is fill my lion mug to the top with
boiling tea.

No Cure
Madison Lawson

Have you heard from Daran today? I send the text as I climb into the car, pulling the seatbelt across my chest. Stretching my neck, I let my eyes close for a second, the weight of the busy day taking its toll.

The reply comes ten minutes later. You didn't hear?

Obviously not. How fucking helpful.

Would I be asking you if I had?

Sorry, I just thought someone would have you called you.

Well they didn't. Why can't she ever just give me a straightforward answer? Karrie, what happened?

He's in the hospital.

Do you ever have those moments when your ears close off, like they just need to take a break for a bit? You know when you play your favorite song and it gets to the end and you realize you didn't hear a single part? Or when you're at a coffee shop, focusing on your work, and the rest of the world has been put on mute?

That's what happens when I read the four-word text.

When I first realized how real the virus was, I was fourteen. Even then, though, it was just like anything else. Not that big of a deal. Dangerous, yes, but mostly controlled. I would be safe. My family would be safe. It was being contained. That's what they told us. Not to worry.

But I saw it in full swing year one of high school. One of the girls in my grade was there one day, smiling and completely healthy, then the next day it was, "Where is Isobel?" "Hospital. She caught the virus."

I didn't know Isobel well. She was just a girl. Tall, pretty, dark and mostly nice. I spoke to her as necessary, nothing more. She was in a different friend group. A smaller one. No one really knew her that well.

Until she caught it. Then suddenly she was the most popular girl in our year. She was everywhere while being nowhere. She was the poster child for friendship. People were crying about what a shame it was in the hallways. People who most likely were the reason she caught it. Carriers.

Her real friends blamed everyone else for her getting sick.

They weren't wrong.

After Isobel, I only knew two others who caught it. One of them didn't die. But they never fully recovered.

Six years later and it's almost unheard of. It still exists, still infects people, but the news doesn't cover it anymore. Until someone already in the spotlight catches it, then it's like the monster that lived under your bed when you were a kid came back for a visit.

Now that I think about it as I'm breaking every traffic law to get to the hospital, the symptoms have been obvious.

I shouldn't have been so ignorant.

I should have seen this happening.

I should have been there for him.

*   *   *

"I like your sweater." My head had snapped up at the unfamiliar voice. An older lady who was standing in front of me in the coffee shop line.

I looked down, forgetting what sweater I was wearing.

'Adams Heritage University'.

I plastered on a smile. "Thank you."

"What year are you?"

"First."

"You must be a smart young man. It's a tough school to get into."

I didn't reply, just nodded curtly and looked back down at my phone.

Hurry up, jackass. Some lady is assuming I'm a genius again. I can sense her wanting to ask more questions. I texted, taking longer than necessary so I had a reason to stare at my phone.

"Waiting for a girlfriend?"

"Roomate," I answered.

She smiled, persistent. "Are you boys in the dorms?" I nodded. This seemed to excite her even more. "Oh, that must be a lot of fun! Really getting the full college experience. Probably lots of late study nights, I assume."

A nod. "He's poli-sci, so he keeps me up and forces me to do my work."

"Well that's good. Having a good study partner is crucial for getting through university."

I gave her a tight smile accompanied by squinted eyes.

I opened my phone again. DUDE, SERIOUSLY.

Walking in, chill.

I read the message and turned, seeing Daran give me his prize winning bitch face.

"Hey, dude."

"Patient, much?"

I shrugged and turned forward. The lady was looking at us with head tilted. I fought the urge to snap at her.

"Is your roommate still coming?" She asked. I lifted my eyebrow and rolled my eyes.

"Hello, I'm Daran." He extended his hand.

She ignored it.

"You're his roommate?"

"Yes, ma'am."

"Oh... Oh! What sport do you play?" My face scrunched further and I reminded myself to stay calm.

Daran didn't miss a beat. "I don't play any sports."

She seemed surprised. "Oh! And you're... political science?"

"Yes ma'am."

"Oh... okay. Well I think that's great! We need more colored young men like you."

She went up to order. Daran sneezed.

*   *   *

Daran was only sick one time during our first year. We thought he just had a bad cold, nothing serious. He got better after a few days staying in bed and forcing me to get him soup. It was a few months after the coffee shop incident and directly after he was almost arrested. I was still in the small convenience store, buying... something irrelevant for this story, and he got a call. He walked out of the store, reaching in his pocket.

I came outside to see a cop asking him to empty his pockets. I stepped in between them.

"Is this even legal?"

"Son, I'm just doing my job."

"Protect and serve, right?" The cop grunted and walked away after that. Daran didn't let me talk about it again.

*   *   *

I hit every red light on the way to the hospital. My foot bounces while I wait at one, eyes darting around, hair rising from the anxiety and fear. At the corner stands a group of club girls.

I remember the night during our second year. The one that made me remember that this virus was still a thing and the people I loved could get infected.

It was a Saturday night and the football team had just won their fifth game in a row. Everyone was celebrating, or at least using that as an excuse to party. I made Daran come with me to a party and promise to DD. He had complained for a moment, saying he had to drive last time, but I just rolled my eyes. We both knew who had more willpower. The first offered drink, and I would give in.

I should have known I was taking him to a petri dish of carriers. I should've protected him.

I was drunk, but I remember the entire night.

I was in the middle of telling this girl, okay I don't remember her name, some story about… something, I honestly don't remember this. But I was talking to her, leaning against the wall, slurring my words yet smirking confidently anyways.

"What was that?" She'd interrupted.

Despite the struggle, I stood up straight and strained to listen.

And then I heard it.

Someone was screaming. A girl. I ran towards the sound, along with No-name and a few other partygoers. I found myself in the middle of the gathering room, the girl who had screamed fallen into some guy's arms, bawling. He grasped her clothes, trying to keep her up, asking her what happened.

She turned and pointed at Daran. I walked towards him, grabbing at his arm, trying and failing to figure out what was happening.

"Him! He tried to... he… he." She threw herself back into her assumed boyfriend's chest, crying more.

A hundred pair of light eyes turned to Daran. A sea of cream skin, pale hair and gritted teeth, screaming at my best friend that he was a monster. Threatening him.

"Dude! Not cool!"

"Get out, dick!"

"I'm going to call the cops."

"I will kill you if you touched her."

"Who even let him in?"

"Hey! Leave him alone!" I yelled. Daran yanked at my arm, trying to shut me up. "He didn't do anything!"

15

"Dude, let's just go," he whispered. "They aren't going to believe you."

Reluctant, I let Daran drag me out of the house. I crossed my arms in the car, eyebrows furrowed and really wanting to punch something.

"What the fuck happened?"

Daran sighed. "Nothing."

"Daran."

"Really, nothing. She was dancing. I was trying to walk through the room and I accidentally bumped into her. She looked at me and started screaming. I didn't even mean to touch her."

I gaped at him. "What a bitch."

"It's fine."

I shook my head. "No, it's not. For all you know she could have been a carrier. She probably was."

"I'm fine. I feel fine."

We get home and that night I rubbed Daran's back while he puked. His skin was clammy with a fever.

I should have realized they were symptoms.

*   *   *

I got tested for the virus before I met Daran. The summer before college, Mom took my sister and I to the doctor for a checkup. We got all the necessary shots and the doctor did a blood test. Routine. Of course it came back negative. I wasn't even a carrier. They say we are usually immune to it. Genetics or something. You're either born with a chance of catching the virus, or you're born without it. The amount of melanin in your body directly affects your chances. The more melanin in your body, the more susceptible you are to catching the virus. I have very little. Daran has a lot.

"You are virus free." The doctor had said. "I also found no detection of you being a carrier, which is good. You won't be a threat to the people around you."

Much of the population was a threat, though. Even if you didn't show any symptoms, you could still be contagious.

Like the lady at the coffee shop. Or the girl at the party. She was probably a carrier. She would live every day of her life and never so much as cough because of the virus. But too much contact with someone like Daran, someone simply born with a virus-prone immune system, and they could die.

Daran could die.

She was just another infection. Just one more interaction to break down his immune system, slowly getting him sicker and sicker. This was probably the breaking point. A slur later and I'm getting the text, 'He's in the hospital.'

I'm out of breath when I run into my sister on the fourth floor. "Where is he?"

"Third room on the right." I'm about to take off

when she grabs my arm. "Look, just… prepare yourself. It's pretty bad." Her words pull at my tears.

She's not wrong. I walk into the small hospital room to see my best friend laying in a bed, soaked in his own sweat, dark skin filled with red, angry patches. "Daran." I gasp.

His eyes struggle to open. When he sees me the smallest of smiles forms. "Hey…"

I grab his hand. "I can't… you…" of course this is when the tears decide to come.

"Hey, it's okay. I'm okay." He says. I scoff.

"No, you're not."

A pause. He swallows, the words hard for him to get out. His head barely shakes. "No… but I… not in pain. The… medicine." I nod, telling him I understand. He doesn't have to finish.

"I should have known. We could have gotten you in here sooner. You could have been treated before it got this bad." I realize this is useless.

It's too late.

My sister walks in then, staying silent by the door. I keep crying. "Daran… you shouldn't be…"

"No one should." He says, smiling again.

I agree. "I can't lose you." He doesn't reply.

I can't lose him. I can't.

I Don't Cry
Hailey Brant

Everything feels like it is going to explode.
All the tears, the rage, the unbearable sadness,
the pure agonizing pain that I have bottled up.
I have bottled it all up because I thought it would be
better
than to feel it all in the moment.

But I was wrong

For now I feel it all at the one singular present that is
me
trying to hold it together
for everyone around me.
Because I am the pillar.

I do not cry.

I do not scream in anguish.

I laugh.

I am not the one who cries.

I am the one who you come to
with tears running down your face,
with anger swirling in your cheeks,
with sharp words to say,
to release before they shred your throat.

I am not the one who cries.

I am your rock,
your comfort,

your happy friend,
whom you vent to
when you need someone to talk to
when you just need to let it out.

And I will always be there for you

But I have bottled up too many emotions.
Too many sad days.
Too many angry words.
Too many things to say.

And I am falling apart

But I can't tell you about it
because you shouldn't have to worry
about me,
about my problems,
about the cracks splintering across my smiling mask.

You don't have to worry

I'm fine

It's nothing but my soul escaping from its bottle.
Nothing but my every sadness pounding against me
like waves upon the rocks
wearing them thinner
and thinner
every day.
Nothing but my anguish
setting fire to my calm forest,
spreading further
and further.
Until nothing is left but ash,
nothing but every raw

piece
of
emotion
trying to drown,
to immolate,
to eviscerate,
to annihilate,
to destroy

me

Don't worry.
It's nothing I haven't dealt with
before.

And now that I have
written down
these tears
these outbursts
these feelings of anguish and sorrow

I will roll them up
into a pretty little scroll
and put them in a bottle

along with the rest.

The Stranger's Camera
Joseph Linscott

What's the scene?

It's summer. July. People are gathered in the streets to celebrate a holiday.

Who's the character? The person of interest?

A boy of a certain, indiscriminant age. Not too old, not too young, but a boy.

What's his focus?

This boy wanders the streets. An idle wanderer to the appearance of all others around him, a flaneur of young age. Yet subtly he moves through the crowd with a certain, discriminant purpose: the girl who has "caught his eye," as they say. We see her in the distance. Blond hair done up with a bow on the top of her head. We cut to her so that she's in focus, not the boy.

Slow motion. She turns around quickly, we just get a glimpse of her blue eyes. We do a quick close up to see that they're looking at the boy. She's looking over at him through the corner of her eye. She's young, like the boy, but not young enough to not wear make up. She's got blush on her cheeks, trying to hide the freckles that are still visible. She looks like she's emulating her mother.

But back to the boy. Every year at this time a massive wandering occurs on the streets of his town, and the boy is no exception. People – those the boy knows, as well as those he does not know – empty out of their houses to maneuver the streets. The stopping and staring at works of art: the deep fried onions, the grilled sausage, the artificially blue icy drink, the ice cream, the themed cans of beer. Staring at the works of celebration. We pan across the crowd – some people with guts, others who are skinny, most everyone is sweating. Cut to some men under a tent grilling sausages. Zoom in to see the beads of sweat on their brows. The stains on their aprons. The dirt under their nails as they flip and stir onions and peppers and sausages around the grill.

Why are they all doing this? How's this boy feel about it?

Why? Freedom, say some. Liberty, others. Pursuit of happiness, the rest. All with a defeated, extinguished breath as they eat their hot dogs and put off the worry of next month's bills. Like most boys who have no conscious experience with these ideologies, the boy typically doesn't care much for everyone's celebration of them – least of which the freedom or the liberty. However, he's old enough this year, his parents said, to go by himself. With newfound freedom he wanders the crowd, seeing the sparklers and sausages with new eyes. This year he can get on board with the pursuit of happiness. Everyone sees him as an idle wanderer like the rest of them, but we frame him as being very much in pursuit. Not the pursuit of the girl in a predator-prey kind of way, he's too young for that to be the purpose. It's a playful pursuit. A truer pursuit of happiness than those around him, so he thinks.

It'll be a play on what it means to be in pursuit of happiness. Capitalistically, happiness means profit — thus the celebration is in the realm of capitalism. The boy's surrounded by this absurd form of pursuit where nobody's pursuing anything for any purpose other than to fill themselves with some sort of feeling that they can't define. We want to contrast that with the boy and his pursuit of his real happiness.

And real happiness is the girl?

So he thinks, and that will have been set up with those memories of him and the girl. As he follows her, he remembers her.

He does?

They've had class together, played at recess together, and had detention together after they were both caught talking in the line to go to recess. In each of these moments there is laughing and smiling. We cut to them giggling in a class room together, repeatedly writing "I will not talk in line" on a piece of paper. Yet they do not know each other outside of school. This is his chance to change that, he thinks.

How long do we follow his wandering pursuit?

A while.

Dialogue?

Very little. Some passing phrases. An oh my god from an exacerbated woman, a heavy guttural ha ha ha from a man, the muffled tones of something that sounds like fuck, and possibly the sounds of children laughing and playing as they run by the boy. Depending on the lighting of the shot the kids will hold sparklers. Around this time of year there's a lot of words being spoken, but not a lot being said, and that's reflected in what can be heard throughout the shot of the boy. We'll get some commonplace phrases to fill the void during the shot – words so unimportant we forget what's been said even as it's being said.

Where's the girl in all of this?

Through this all we follow the boy in this pursuit. We'll shoot from behind the boy. We mostly see the back of his head. He stays in the center of the shot. We keep her in the shot as often as possible – we have to see that she's his pursuit. The girl will be wearing something to stand out from the crowd. They'll be wearing mostly reds and blues and whites – we'll make the shades bright and vibrant. An assault of freedom we could call it. When people pass by the camera, blocking him from our view, his presence will still be felt because she will be in the distance. She will wear black to contrast. Her blond hair and her American flag bow telling us we're still with him. So we can see her. So we can know the boy is looking at her.

While some around him wander and stop to take in the food and the art, the boy wanders without stopping. His wandering takes a direct route. And we keep our gaze directly on him as his gaze lays on the girl.

When does the boy catch up to her?

It takes time. He gets stopped along the way.

By what?

A family friend. We'd know it's a family friend because they'll say something like "you're growing up to look just like your father" or something along those lines. Something that will sound more natural. Maybe it's an actual friend of the boy? Regardless it has to be a phrase everyone would know. People should be able to respond to the phrase as though it were a question because they all know the answer that must be given when someone says a familiar phrase. Something so common it's forgotten even as it's remembered. It'll be a phrase so natural people won't even know that they didn't hear the boy respond to it.

So the boy gets stopped and he loses track of the girl. We see him panic. He can't find her. He starts hopping up and down to try and see her over the crowd. The camera tracks his view as he turns and turns, three-hundred-sixty degrees, but alas there's no black in the crowd, no blond hair with a bow that is distinctly the girl's. So his wandering becomes transparent to those around him. We start to see them looking at him strangely, like they know he's not wandering like the rest of them. A middle-aged man holding a beer and a sausage stares, mouth open with bits of greasy bread stuck to the sides of his mouth. The man's daughter, holding a hot dog and a soda, emulates her father's expression. They know he's in pursuit of something. More and more, as he moves through the crowd, we see their upturned noses and looks of disgust which they direct at him. Two men in the process of exchanging goods glare at the boy – both hands in a frozen tug-of-war with sausage and money. They're offended that he would pursue happiness while the rest of them are wandering in idle profiteering.

Then eventually they stop moving out of his way. They start blocking him. The shot turns to black-and-white – an homage to The Twilight Zone. The boy spins around. Everyone's looking at him. Zoom in on a clenched fist. He tries to fight it at first. Zoom in on gritted teeth. He gives in. Zoom in on a tiny trampled American flag. He let's their bodies determine his body. He takes himself off the tracks of his pursuit. He walks in an indiscriminant manner. The boy buys himself a blue icy drink. The others around him start to lose their disgusted faces and go back to their own wanderings. We stay on him as he stands still, holding the cup in his hand, occasionally sipping through the straw. We only get the shot from behind to start, then we slowly rotate around to a close up on his face. We see his eyes darting back and forth. We pan out and he drops the cup and starts to run through the crowd.

We track him from behind, pushing people out of his way who are trying to stop him. Some what the's and hey's get shouted from the crowd but the boy keeps running. Eventually he gets grabbed by an old lady wearing a white American flag shirt. She glares at the boy. We cut to her makeup – her mascara, her eye shadow, her lipstick – then to her jewelry – her earrings, her necklace – then to her bracelet, wrapped around the wrist which leads to the hand which is holding the boy. There's a short struggle between the two. He gets free from her hold and continues his run before more people can get to him.

When he clears himself through the crowd, he's stopped in his tracks.

The girl in black is no longer wearing black. She's no longer a contrast to the rest of the crowd. We realize she had been wearing a dark blue. She was part of the crowd. And the boy sees her kissing another boy. Another boy who is wearing black. We get the memory of the boy and girl in the classroom laughing. They look at each other and smile. Cut to the image of a dark, shadowy figure in the corner of the classroom. We get the memory of them playing on the playground, laughing, looking at each other and smiling. Cut to the image of a dark, shadowy figure in the distance behind them. We get the memory of them giggling in detention writing the same phrase repeatedly. However, this time the phrase is "Kissing another. Not me." The dark, shadowy figure sitting in a desk behind them.

Back in the crowd, we move the shot so that we rotate around to see his face. By the look of confusion we get from him we can tell he doesn't know this other boy. His adolescent pursuit has suddenly turned sexual. And he has lost. We move away from him a bit and see that the boy is wearing a white shirt. The shot continues so that as we rotate to get another shot of the back of his head.

The scene changes.

We're back where we started and the boy has gotten older.

But he's still a boy. Adolescence is a wide-ranging term, and he takes advantage of that. It's why he's back home. It's why we always come back home. We want freedom, liberty, and the pursuit of happiness until we need our parents again.

The only way to look back on time is through a stranger's camera. That's how we view our earlier experiences. We are still technically an adolescent, though we've aged many years and feel nothing like our earlier adolescence.

After summers we go back to school, we laugh and giggle and play and look at other girls and boy, and then one day we go to college. Unless we don't. But I did. And after college, when things don't go well we come back home, to live with our parents. Like I did.

I'm uncomfortably standing here, in that same part of town, during that same time of year. I am free, I am liberated, and I have no happiness for which to pursue. I see that this town has changed very little from that film I play back in my mind. Yet, like all acquaintances filtered through our perceptions from memory, very little seems to have changed.

I wander the streets, taking in the fried onion rings and grilled sausages and icy blue drinks, a drink which I have once again bought. The children are laughing and screaming and running with sparklers. Music from a nearby bandstand is cascading the street in melody, while the oh my god's and ha ha ha's, and the muffled fuck, from adults buzz in and out. I could be an adult, but I'm not.

I hear from behind my name called out. A person I once knew whose life, so far removed in time from when we could say we truly knew each other, I cannot even begin to imagine what they are like and who they are now. We say some passing phrases, within the phrases could be found some questions, yet we both choose to ignore them and not answer. We both say that it has been good to see each other, though I assume neither of us has thought what it would mean for it to be bad to have seen each other, and we depart.

As I watch him walk away I notice someone in the distance. Someone who has been behind me as I've wandered through this crowd. They are wearing white and they are looking at me. I replay memories that we could have shared – the classroom, the playground, detention – but I know that they are false. I do not remember them.

I turn around in hopes that they, like me, are just wandering. Though with their presence I am no longer wandering. Unlike my memory, no one around seems to notice or take offense. I do not hurry myself through the crowd. I keep a modest pace that's set with those around me. I do not push anyone. I move the crowd with my body – this is liberation. Once I get through to a sparser section of people I am free. I turn around to see if this other person has made progress in their pursuit.

They are gone. Or they have caught up. And I am unable to tell the difference.

Nanette
Taylor Mogul

Nanette felt uneasy sitting on the bus as it took her home from school. She always felt distressed on the ride home. Once, in the 2nd grade she had missed the stop at her road. She had figured she would get off at the next stop and walk back, but she failed to realize that the next stop wasn't for another 8.4 miles (an unreasonable distance for a 7 year old to walk alone). In her embarrassment she chose to wait and see if perhaps the route would loop back around, but it did not, and Nanette had to sit up front with the frustrated bus driver (who smelled strongly of moth balls) for 21 minutes to get back to her stop. Despite being an entire year ago, she still was desperate to not let that happen again. At every stop Nanette noted how much longer it would be until she needed to get off, and was careful not to get distracted by the other kids on the bus. As the bus slowed to a stop at Elm Street 6 stops to go, she noticed that Timothy, her next-door neighbor, began to get up to leave. She panicked. Timothy and I always get off at the same stop. Maybe there's something wrong with our road and we need to get off early. I should get off now just in case. She started shifting her things, getting ready to leave, when she noticed that Timothy was getting off with Shane. Timothy's parents are going away for the long weekend and Tim is going to stay with his cousin Shane. She remembered. It's fine, still 6 more stops. When her stop finally came up she quickly exited the bus, and crossed the road to her street. She could see her house sitting quietly at the end of the road. Usually this is when her uneasiness began to lift, but it stayed. It was especially strange given the upcoming weekend. Getting off the bus on a Friday was typically the most invigorating feeling, but today, the closer she walked home, the more her stomach began to sink. She tried to shake this feeling by reminding herself of all the fun things she would be doing this weekend Barbie Gymnastics CD-ROM, raking leaves and then leaping into them, reading the rest of the new Harry Potter book, but her uplifting thoughts simmered away as she stepped into her driveway and a slow chill worked its way up her spine. Despite the nippy air beginning to soak into her skin, she did not want to go inside the house, but knowing that her mother's warm smile was waiting for her was enough of a convincer in spite of her vague dread.

It was quiet. Her younger sister was typically in the kitchen sneakily snacking on whatever after school treat their mother had prepared for Nanette, but there was neither her scavenger sister, nor sustenance.

Nanette went to look for someone, even her torturous sister, to say hello to, to bring her back to reality, to remind her that everything is the same as it's always been, and that her unsettled feeling is rooted in nothing but her imagination. There was nobody to be found, however. She called throughout the house, looked in all the rooms, yet there was no one. Nanette's alarm was growing and growing when suddenly a wave of relief washed over her. They probably went out for an errand! Mom's car will not be in the garage, and that will mean that she will be home shortly. She went out to the garage to confirm this for herself, but somehow she knew that she wouldn't find an empty bay, but her mother's car sitting inside it. The trunk was open and grocery bags were still sitting there. She peeked in them and found melted ice cream and warm milk. She didn't know whether to feel relieved, or scared. On one hand, this meant that her mother was home, on the other hand, she could not find her mother or sister anywhere, and the groceries that had been left out for at least a couple hours was very concerning. The distraction of figuring out this mystery was at least keeping her from feeling total dread, until she heard a loud thump come from the basement. She hadn't checked the basement – it is not so surprising that she hates it down there, it's not only damp and musty, which agitates her allergies, but it's dark and bare. She did not want to check the basement, but the hopes that her mother was there, just happily doing laundry was enough to push her comfort zone about 8 feet down the stairs. She grabbed a flashlight and crept slowly down the steep wooden steps, careful to hold onto the railing. As she reached the cold, concrete floor she turned the flashlight on and shone it around the hollow space. The only light that lit the entire basement was a lone bulb hanging from the ceiling in the middle of the large room. As she worked her way towards it, she swept the area with the thin beam of light from her dimming lantern. She saw nothing aside from the old washer and dryer, and dust particles drifting through the air. She finally reached the long string for the light, and shakily tugged it down. The intense brightness from the bare bulb was too much for her eyes, and she squinted them shut, and brought her hands up to her face, dropping her flashlight in the process. It was then when she heard another thump. This time louder and much closer than the muffled one she heard from the garage, she gathered the courage to open her eyes and she saw her mother standing about ten feet away, not moving, with a toothy smile painted onto her face, but her eyes held no joy.

"Mom?"

No response.

"Mom, hey, where's Paulie?"

Her mother started walking closer towards her, but her steps were short and they dragged on the floor, like an old woman's steps. Nanette heard her sister giggle, but she wasn't sure where she heard it from. In the empty basement the sound seemed to echo endlessly all around her. She backed away slowly from her towards the stairs, but her mother had reached the light, and as she pulled the string, before her world was

plunged into darkness, Nanette could swear that she
saw her mother's eyes turn black.

Absent Taiga
Cody Huffman

The thin, metal roof shook and rattled above. The constant, sporadic knocking of the loose shutters against the crooked, pine wood house disguised itself as an angry intruder at the door. The wind sounded like air blowing through a straw, only a hundred times harder, swirling around the simple shelter as if it was trapped in the center of a tornado. Snowflakes the size of plastic plates pelted everything that stood from the Earth's ground. He usually didn't wake during these ungodly storms, but for some reason, he did that night. It could have been the particular severity of that storm, but it was more likely to be from the nightmarish starvation.

The man sat up from his silk-lined blankets to grab the old bag of beef jerky that was sitting half-opened on the dresser at his feet. There were only three pieces left. He moved his pale, dirty fingers around the pieces petrified meat, sifting through them, as if the act was somehow adding more to the bag. After he ate the remaining pieces, he took several deep gulps of water from his jug and went back to sleep. The storm continued until it the sun creeped over the tops of the cedar and pine trees on the hill that looked down onto the tiny house.

The alarm clock on his watch went off at 10 A.M.,

which startled him. He had just recently found another battery for it after living without one for a while. He had accustomed to letting the sunlight wake him. The occasional sounds of howls never failed, either. He rose out of bed and examined himself in the frozen window directly in front of him. His makeshift wolf hide coat had become tattered and worn as the stitching started to loosen and holes formed across the back. The dark grey fur of the used-to-be wolf had paled over time.

The man wiped his greasy, dark brown hair over the side of his head, brushing it out of his eyes. He had just recently cut a few inches off of his hair with an old pair of rusty scissors he found in the trunk of one of the broken down cars outside on the main road. Even though he had no one to share his new haircut with, he was still proud of it in a way. His stomach made an almost inaudibly low rumble, begging him for substance. He took a few swigs of water and then searched his hiking pack for any sort of food and energy. The can of sardines that he had seen the night before was empty; making him feel stupid at the fact that he only saw the side of the can and figured it was unopened and full.

The fire in the black, metal stove had been dead for a few hours, at least. He didn't mind much because he didn't have anything to cook anyway. The single-roomed house was still slightly warm from last night's fire. Outside, gusts of screaming wind echoed through the forest behind the cabin and all the way to the seemingly infinite, frozen ocean that sat across the main road.

"At least the storm is gone...for now," he said with a sigh. He cleared his throat, tightened the laces on his deer skin boots, grabbed his rifle, and went back to the window looking out to the white world that waited for him. He couldn't see much because the window was more ice than it was glass, which made for a blurry sight. The only things he was looking for were blackish-grey bodies of mass moving across the surfaces. The coast seemed to be clear for his trek across the snow.

He had been living in that house for about three weeks. He starved the area from all of the potential resources it had held. He had picked all of the lichen from the limbs of the nearby trees, scavenged every container that resided in a mile radius, and fished the fishing hole he had cut open empty. It was time for him to continue his journey across the coast line, temporarily settling in any and every house he came across along the way. He opened the front door to the house and stuck his gaunt face out to get a better view of his surroundings. Other than the whistling wind and rustling of the thousands of branches around him, no other sound could be heard.

All of his belongings were in his travel pack, which was more than half the height of him. The length of the bag went from the tip of his red toboggan, all the way past his wolf coat and down to the base of his buttocks, which were covered with layers of long-johns he had found in various closets and dresser drawers, topped off with more skinned deer hides. He became very skilled at making clothes from the cured hides he collected. Those hides were the only things saving him from the piercingly cold temperatures. Unless there was a storm, he didn't really get cold while wearing them. He came a long way since the beginning of the end. At first, he was slowly freezing to death, struggling to find even a suitable down jacket. Now, he was creating his own protective clothing with thread and a fishing hook.

He started on the main road, a highway, heading east. He didn't venture too far during his scavenging runs so most of the area was new to him after about twenty minutes of walking. An hour's walk took him three because of the constant searching for materials. He always hesitated before going into a newly found house because of the fear of what might be waiting for him on the inside. A wild animal may have slipped in through a busted or opened window, the floor may be rotted and cave in on him, or the ultimate fear of finding what he had been resentfully searching for all along, a living person.

He hadn't seen a breathing person in what felt like fifteen years, but, in reality, was only around three or four years. The last person he had approached pulled a 12-gauge shotgun on him. The man was older, maybe late sixties or early seventies, with snow white eye brows and thinning hair. One of his eyes was an icy blue color, while the other was tar black. The old man shot before he was close enough to yell his own name, which did nothing but attract a curious pack of wolves to his approximate location.

While searching through another small house along the highway, he found a sealed can of dog food. His hazel eyes widened as if he had just won the lottery. In his mind, it was as pleasing as if he had won. His stomach was pleading with him to eat at that moment, but the food was far too cold. He threw the can into his backpack and continued out of the house and down the road. He eventually walked to a tall, concrete beamed bridge with two totaled cars sitting, facing each other like they were paying respects at a funeral. He was walking on the right side of the bridge with his black glove gliding across the top of the handrail, making a tiny snowstorm as he went. He looked over the edge and saw something green lodged in the snow below him, halfway under the bridge.

He got to the end of the bridge, turned right, and slid down the snowy hill, crouched like some sort of ice surfer. Upon closer inspection, it was a green jacket collar poking out of the snow. He scratched and clawed at the snow, sending it in every direction around him.

"Ah, shit," he whispered under the whimpering wind. He uncovered the body of an unfortunate soul, a middle-aged woman, face down with two broken legs. She must've fallen off the bridge some while ago. Perhaps one of the heavy storms caught her by surprise as she was on a loot run and she walked right off the side of the bridge. One couldn't see their hand in front of them in one of those storms. The snow would have covered her up within an hour of her death. Her skin was puffy and black and had the feeling of cold wood. Her appendages were nearly frozen solid, unable to be moved. Her head was somewhat smaller than normal. It looked like some sort of bird had picked most of the back of her head clean, leaving nothing but her beige, scratched skull and a few scattered pieces of scalp and skin with long, black hair matted to them.

The man reached into his backpack, pulled out two cedar logs, some matches, and some fire accelerator. He placed the logs less than a foot away from the body, positioning them in a way to try to block the light wind coming from the south. He sprayed the logs with a couple ounces of accelerator and threw a match on top.

"I'm sorry, but I have to do this," he said with such anguish. He took out his knife and placed it at his side in the snow. He pulled out an old, blackened frying pan and the metal stand that he had used so many times before. With the occasional squirt of accelerator, the fire started roaring, growing in size. It soon melted away all of the snow that was still on top of the body. He pulled the body closer to him and the fire, until her

42

left arm was almost lying on top of it. The visible skin on her arm started to shine from the water of the melted snow. He took his glove off of his right hand and wrapped his skinny fingers around her swollen black forearm. Her skin was still cold, but wasn't nearly as hard. It was more squishy, like a stress ball. There were ridges left on her forearm where his fingers had squeezed, like tiny mountains made of coal expanding over the Earth.

After a while, he stripped off her clothes. There wasn't one inch of her body that wasn't charred black. A disgusting sight. The thought of the act that was about to take place almost made his stomach stop growling, as if the hunger was retreating back into the deep depths of his body. But he knew that his hunger wasn't silenced. He needed to do this because he never knew when his next meal would be. He took slices of the pale, grey meat that he cut and placed them neatly on one side of the pan. The smell of rotten flesh and garbage danced around him. He grabbed the can of dog food from his backpack, opened it, and let it sit over the fire for a few minutes until it was able to be poured onto the pan.

"What a meal," he said to himself in disgust. It was a dreadful dinner, but it did what it had to do. After he was done eating, he took water from some melted snow and washed out his frying pan, wiping it clean with a scrap of her pants. He packed up all of his belongings and climbed back up the hill he had slid

43

own. The sunlight had gotten dimmer as it was later in the day. In the distance, across the frozen ocean, was a small island. On the island sat a red lighthouse with a massive billboard-sized Canadian flag flapping on the side. He had been to a lighthouse several months before. Because the last one was so densely packed with supplies, he knew he had to make the trip.

The man started walking along the highway to try to get more parallel with the island. He didn't get a hundred feet before he heard the howls of a hungry predator. The echo swirled around his head and into his ears, stabbing his brain with a freezing spike of fear. He stopped walking and crouched behind the lip of the highway. Above him, on the hill beside the road, were two massive wolves. They must've smelled the dinner. One was darker than the other and much more muscular. The other one was visibly younger and sicklier looking.

It wasn't possible for him to continue along the road. He reluctantly started across the ice directly towards the lighthouse. He always tried to avoid the ice as much as possible, only going on it to fish when needed. Even when he did, he only went a few feet out from the snow. Behind him, the dogs were still there up on the hill. The smaller of the two was sitting down while the larger one was pacing back and forth as if looking for trouble. The man kept walking tentatively like he was crossing on a narrow beam. The ice was at least a few inches thick, but he was still nervous. He weighed somewhere around a hundred and seventy pounds and the backpack with all of his gear sat at around sixty, along with his ten pound rifle; a fair amount of pressure on something as delicate as ice.

The daily fog had rolled in, making it very difficult to see. For once, he was happy it came. If he couldn't see the wolves, surely they couldn't see him. The howls slowly became less and less audible has he approached the island. The occasional crack in the ice made his hungry heart skip a few beats, causing him to stutter-step. The fog had gotten so thick that the lighthouse had disappeared. He continued walking north from the road. It took him around half an hour to reach the island. The night sky had just appeared when he climbed up the hill to the lighthouse. The mixture of darkness and fog forced him to pull out his lantern to find the door.

Inside the lighthouse, he found several cans of food, wooden chairs and tables that he could use for burning material, and some old shirts which would make good bandages. He took most items out of his bag and sat them on the floor around the desks and dresser. There was another stove for him to cook food and boil water in. A picture rested on the dresser of a man and woman holding each other and smiling. He picked it up and studied it, taking in every feature of their faces. He folded it in half and placed it in his back pocket.

Mirrors
Hallie Trader

There's a certain time of night – after you've been riding for hours, after you've drifted in and out of sleep a few times – when the light of the stars blend with distant headlights, and one simply doesn't care to make the distinction between the two. The exhaustion of the trip surrounded my mind; it had tried its hardest to hypnotize me, to pull my attention to what I wasn't sure were stars or headlights. The bus had been practically silent for over an hour, save for someone snoring towards the back. We'd come to a straight-stretch of highway, a seemingly endless lull of concrete.

It should have been enough to put me to sleep, but the weight of guilt and shame were too heavy on my conscience. I couldn't think of sleep; I could only think of her face, and how it broke under the force of my heated words. I could only think of how badly I wanted to reel my words back to me – take them back so they could no longer attack her, take them away so she wouldn't retaliate. But I couldn't.

Our problems were not new; we'd been bickering verbally and hating each other silently for months. Makenzie and I fought diplomatically – we formed teams, did things in polite ways, never raised our voices – but everyone knew we were always on the edge of killing each other. No one really understood why, though. It didn't make sense; we should have gotten along. We had the same interests (the only reason we met was theater), the same sense of humor, the same insecurities. By all reasonable logic, we should have been best friends. The only problem was the fact that we wished the other had never been born.

I hated her and everything she did. Makenzie was the bane of my existence, and I'm sure I was hers as well. But I had to put up with her. The only way of avoiding her would have been dropping out of theater, and that was the only thing I refused to do – so we fought. All the time, we fought.

In the beginning the arguments weren't so bad. They started with quiet, snide comments that made our blood boil, and envision the best ways to humiliate the other. It wouldn't have escalated to that point, but it was fun to fantasize about. After a while, however, the tension built. Eventually we forgot about being classy and just yelled at each other over pointless things. I think it would have escalated beyond control a lot sooner than it did, but then the International Thespian Society called.

Our group had won a contest, they said. They were sending us to Nationals, the International Thespian Festival, free of charge, and we would be performing in front of thousands. Instantly, all conflict within the group dissolved in the excitement... or so we thought.

The festival took place in Lincoln, Nebraska in the middle of a heat wave. It took eighteen hours on a bus full of teenagers to get there, and by the time we made it to our rooms, even the closest of friends were too crabby to be nice to each other. Obviously, it was a recipe for disaster.

Everyone had some sort of problem during the week. A birthday was ruined, a couple broke up, and it was generally too hot to enjoy much of anything. Finally though, "dance night" came. All of the girls were all excited – we spent two hours getting ready. Makenzie and her friends had spent the week avoiding me and mine, but that night was different; everyone was being civil. We were getting ready together. We were bonding, because this dance was the most important thing in the world. But then we got dressed.

What happened next was stereotypical, and I'm ashamed of it. Makenzie and I put on our dresses, and turned around to face each other. And then all hell broke loose.

"Just what do you think you're wearing?" she asked, and I could practically feel the acid dripping off the words. She was wearing a tight, low-cut, red thing – and it was all too similar to mine.

I could feel the rage I'd built up about to spill over. I could almost taste the loathing I had for this girl. Who did she think she was? She'd made my life hell for months and she had the audacity to be mad about a dress? My palms dampened. I could feel the fire beneath my cheeks. And before I could control myself, before I could calm myself down, she said to me, "I said, 'What do you think you're wearing?'"

It was a simple question. But her voice shook with rage... her words were like daggers and she threw them straight at my face. And I broke.

I don't remember much of what I said to her. I don't remember much of what she said to me. I don't remember much of anything except the white-hot rage of two teenage girls who wanted nothing more than to hurt each other. She called me a "dirty skank" and said I was a bad actress. I told her she was a low-life who belonged in a ditch somewhere, not the stage. The goal was tears. The weapons were words. The soldiers fought hard and attacked until we realized how our audience had changed. The girls around us, who had been happy and friendly only five minutes ago, now looked at us with contempt. There was disappointment drawn across their faces. In an instant, it had been decided – Makenzie and I weren't worthy of their friendship anymore. Not then, anyway.

We stopped. Nobody moved. For once, this group of people who were never quiet, never calm, stood and stared in complete silence. Makenzie and I froze, staring at each other, realizing the awful things we had said to each other. The goal had been humiliation. The weapons had been insults. The soldiers had been successful, but we had both lost the war...

I wasn't sure where we were then; I could have sworn that trip had lasted seven years, not seven days. The road was unchanging, a solid, straight line that didn't seem to ever end. I couldn't help but wonder how we got to that point. Honestly, I had no idea how any of it happened. I couldn't have told you why we hated each other so much...

 And then it hit me; this boulder of realization hit me so hard it rolled right over me, leaving me stunned and flat. Makenzie was stubborn, hot headed, bossy, sly, cruel in the nicest way... But while all those things were true about her, I realized they were also entirely true in a description of me. The truth of it slapped me in the face. The sting of knowing that the only reason I hated this girl so much was because I saw all of my negative qualities in her was almost too much to handle. And then I realized that that's why she hated me too. We saw ourselves mirrored in the other and we lashed out against it. The knowledge sat in my stomach like a rock. I looked out the window, not sure if I was looking at a constellation or a Sedan...

 The light of the stars that night blended with headlights. The road seemed like it would never end; it seemed like nothing could ever change. Of course, everyone knows stars and headlights aren't the same thing. Everyone knows the road eventually curves. It took a while, but I eventually realized that Makenzie and I had similar attributes, but we weren't the same person.

We were stars and headlights – confused for each other, but very different. Our relationship did eventually change, as the roads we traveled finally curved and forked away from each other. However, that night, when the pain was still fresh and the shame still hung from my chest like a scarlet letter, it didn't seem like the road would ever end. I fell asleep believing the headlights on the hill were stars.

The Mountain
Aaron Radcliff

Terrain is always an issue when conducting a mission. If you don't know the lay of the land, you could easily end up at a tactical disadvantage. And that's the trouble with terrain: It always changes. Sure, you don't have mountains rising and falling like the tides, but you have wind. You have rain. You have sunlight. It all plays a factor in how well things go. One miscalculation and you can have a serious problem on your hands, and problems are something that I prefer to do without.

I looked over to my right and could see Walker setting up his equipment. It'd taken us hours to get up this mountain and to find the perfect overwatch position. No clouds, no rain, clear view. We'd been traveling for the better part of the day. Wake up at 0600, gear up and move out by 0715, arrival at destination by 1500. We had requested to be airlifted into the mountain range in order to preserve our energy but HQ wouldn't grant it. Best we can do is drop you within six clicks they told us. Secrecy was the main priority of this mission. I understood though. Didn't mean I had to like it.

The wind started to pick up coming from the east. Gentle, but just enough to severely offset any shots we'd need to make. I heard Walker sigh and swear to himself as he readjusted the blind for us to lie under. The wind had tipped over the peg and ended up knocking everything down. Eventually though, he had it set back up and we took our positions. Me the sniper, Walker the spotter.

It's a beautiful weapon the M2010 ESR. Bolt-action, shoulder-fired weapon capable of discharging a .300 Winchester Magnum effectively up to 1,300 yards fitted with top-of-the-line telescopic sight and AAC sound suppressor. They hammered that into our heads day in and day out. Well, they did back when we were still using the Barrett M82 in training a few years back, different specifications for the weapons aside. Now, it's just good practice to know everything you can about your weapon. It's an extension of you. An extension of your arm, eye, mind, soul. An extension of the hand of Death. Some morbid, cold-blooded stuff they though drilling into our minds would make us hardened. Worked for some, not so much for me.

We weren't strictly on military business. It's meant to be off-record UN work. Me, Walker, and two others. French guys, of course. I don't know why, but they always feel compelled to pair us with French guys. It's not like they don't know what they're doing but I would just feel a bit more comfortable with other Americans. We train together, live together, and wait to get home to our families together. Is it so much to ask to work with somebody we see as family? I suppose so.

The French always struck me as a bunch of smug

cunts, too.

"Hey, Connor?" I heard Walker say. He took his face away from his spotting scope and proceeded to reach into his pocket and grab a pack of gum. Three years I've worked with him and he always had some on him.

"Want some?"

"No thanks, Walker."

"Come on, man. It's been, what, three, four years? Call me Danny."

"I'll remember that when we get back, Sergeant."

"Oh my God, that's worse than you calling me 'Walker.' At least that's my actual name. You know, because I'm a human, not a rank. So, what are we doing out here again?"

"You really need to pay more attention in the mission briefs, Walker. They have information vital to the-"

"Jesus Christ, Connor. You're so by-the-book. It's sickening. If I wanted to have somebody regurgitate my life failings back at me in a tone like that, I'd just go back home and listen to my dad tell me about how I was the least favorite out of the three kids. Just answer the damn question and spare me ass reaming, ok?"

He's a nice guy, honestly. We've spent so much time together, been on so many missions together, that he was more family to me than my actual brother and sister. But he also knew how to get on my nerves. There's a time and place for being flippant and lighthearted, but a mission isn't the place. I wish he'd realize that sometimes

"We're here to provide overwatch for operatives Lefevre and Molyneux, code name Juliet 6-4. There's been some intel coming in that members of the regime have been committing acts of violence toward the populace and that they may be gearing up for possible combat operations. Rather than send in the U.S., the UN opted for low-key reconnaissance missions and would decide based on their findings whether or not to proceed with sanctions and military action," I told him, making no effort to hide the annoyance in my voice.

"Fun shit. So, whatcha think? Coup, invasion, or false info? Five dollars says it's a coup starting up. Libya, Bosnia, all the fun places have coups."

"Bosnia wasn't a coup, Walker. It was attempted annexation. What's the time right now?"

"Oh excuse me, Mr. Know-It-All. It's about 1545, maybe 1600. But it looks watch stopped working. Battery must be dead. So, who knows?"

I sighed and grabbed the radio from my rucksack and began to fiddle with the knobs. Working one of these was never my strong suit. I always ended up having to just twist and turn the knobs until it eventually worked or found someone who actually knew what they were doing. Even though Walker's watch was dead, it was still past the time allotted for the second team to radio in. Maybe it's just my anal personality but I can't help but feel like things always go wrong when people don't radio in on time. It's that inability to know where your men or other squads are that make conducting missions difficult.

"Juliet 6-4, this is Juliet 2-5. Do you copy?"

Silence. I wasn't too surprised. You can stand beside a satellite on top of Mt. Everest on a clear day and still not get a functioning signal. I twisted the knobs and radioed again. Nothing. I must've been doing something wrong, but instead, I decided to adjust the signal and radio back to base. Maybe we were given incorrect frequencies.

"HQ-actual, this is Juliet 2-5. Do you copy?"

"Juliet 2-5, this is HQ-actual copying. Proceed with transmission."

"HQ-actual, what're the transmission frequencies for Juliet 6-4? We failed to receive any transmission or signal from them by 1530. I've tried them on multiple occasions on 126.2 as instructed and haven't heard a thing."

"Juliet 2-5 those are the proper frequencies. If you can't raise them, there's nothing we can do. Radio back upon mission completion. And remember 2-5, if mission becomes compromised, break comms and call in on your satellite phone provided. HQ-actual out."

"Juliet 2-5 out. Fuck."

"Don't worry, Connor," I heard Walker say, "When the French fries get to where they need to be, they'll let us know. For now, get snuggled in. We could be here a while."

As we laid down and took our positions, I reached into my shoulder pocket and pulled out my favorite picture. Despite its faded color and frayed edges, the smile of the woman and child could illuminate even the darkest room. Carmen, her hair dark and flowing around her olive-kissed skin. Jennifer, the gap between her teeth seemed more adorable every time I looked at her. Her hair was in its natural bouncing red curls that would hang below her bright green eyes. Her mother and I never figured out how Jennifer managed to look absolutely nothing like us, but it didn't matter.

"Jenny-bean starts kindergarten this year, right?" Walker said.

Hurriedly, I put the picture back into my pocket. "Yeah," I responded.

"I'm sorry, man. We'll be done soon though. You

think Carmen would make some of her famous roast chicken when we get home? I know how much she loves cooking that."

"Walker, if any food that tastes like an overcooked sponge constitutes your idea of 'famous,' then I can't imagine what kind of other shit you eat."

"Man, it's better than the fucking DFAC," he said, laughing.

He was right. Anything was better than the food here, better than anything around here. Even Carmen's cooking.

*

The sun had started to go down behind the ridge of the mountains, but it was still clear enough to see. No radio chatter, no ambient noises other than the sounds of our breathing. They say that you need to have the mind of a killer to do this job. I'd say that having the patience of a saint would be most important.

In the valley below us a rumbling began to rise. It echoed off the mountains and through the trees, but it was obvious to me what it was: Humvee.

"Walker, get me eyes on that valley. We've got a Humvee coming in."

Adjusting himself and pressing his scope to his

eyes, Walker began to scan the valley as the Humvee pulled out of the trees and into the clearing. We were the only people in this area who knew of this mission. This Humvee and whoever is in it can't be friendly. Thankfully, we were high enough up to not be spotted. Or so I hoped.

"Yo, Connor, we've got some guys stepping out. I've got seven guys and they look like they're part of the regime. They're strapped too, looks like four with AK's, two snipers, and one with what looks like an AT4. Seems a bit heavy for out here, don't you think?"

I reached into my pocket and pulled out the satellite phone and dialed the only preset number. I waited forever for anything to happen, but nothing did. Nobody left the Humvee, nobody made a sound. This didn't make any sense.

It took forever, but eventually, the call patched through. Captain Weber answered. Whenever that happened, it was never good. We all knew that.

"Captain Weber, it's Staff Sergeant Connor. Can you hear me alright?"

"I've got you loud and clear, Connor. You know this line is only for broken comms or compromised missions, so you better have a good goddamn reason for calling me on it. You better hope to hell it's the first."

I hoped so too.

"Sir, we've got seven in the valley. All unfriendly and one has an anti-tank weapon. We have yet to receive any transmissions from Juliet 6-4. I think-"

"Oh, fuck. Connor, you need to see this," Walker suddenly said. "It's 6-4."

I raised my rifle and adjusted my scope. Standing in front of the Humvee were all seven members with two men kneeling in front of them. Dark green fatigues with faces painted black and a small blue symbol on their shoulders. It was them.

"Sir, we have visual on Juliet 6-4. They're currently under the possession of the soldiers from the Humvee. I repeat we have visual on 6-4, mission is compromised. Request permission to engage and attempt rescue of 6-4."

"Negative," I heard him say. It wasn't at all the answer I expected or wanted.

"Sir?"

"Negative, Connor. We aren't even supposed to be here. If you engage without being fired on first, it could be considered an act of war. Besides, there's only two of you. You may have the high ground, but you're still outnumbered. You cannot engage. Do you understand me? 6-4 is compromised, don't compromise yourself as well. Fall back to prior established drop zone and await pickup. Roger?"

"Yes, sir."

I hung up the phone and turned to Walker. I could see the look on his face. He didn't have to hear both ends of the phone call to know what I had been told. He looked down at the ground and me, and then back to the valley.

"We have to engage, Connor. You know we have to."

"Are you serious? There's seven of them and two of us. Even if we had been granted permission and could fight them off, there's no way that we'd be able to save 6-4. We'd get one shot off and then they'd be executed. You know that just as well as I do."

"What I know is that we have two guys down there who are part of this mission. We can't go back without them."

"We have to."

"We have to? Sure, fine. Then we can go back and try to sleep. We can go home and make a quick stop in Paris and tell these guys' families how we 'did what we could.' Lie to their face and tell them that we couldn't save their sons when you and I both know we could. Is that what you want?"

61

"Danny, you know that's not what I-"

"What if it was you? Would you want to be down there, knowing people could save you and instead leaving? Would you want them to go home to Carmen, to Jennifer, and tell them you never had a chance? You were never given one? Would you want that? Because I sure as shit wouldn't. We have to at least try for Christ's sake. And if you won't then I will."

Walker reached to his side and pulled up his weapon. The M4 carbine. He only had one magazine with twenty rounds. He and I both knew this.

"Danny, you know you couldn't do it on your own, even if I let you."

"Then stay here and help me. The least we could do is try. They don't know we're here. For all they know, they're being shot at by rebels or some shit, not Americans. We're soldiers. Snipers. We swore to protect our brothers and comrades, no matter what. That doesn't change here."

I stared at him and then at my rifle. I looked back at him and saw extend an extended fist waiting for me to tap mine to it. His mind was made up. He wasn't leaving no matter what. I shrugged him off and pulled up my rifle. He was right, but we couldn't do it. We shouldn't. I looked back to Walker and back to the valley.

"So, are you with me?" he said.

If I'm a good person then I deserve so much better but if I'm a bad person I deserve so much worse
Alex Wilson

I'm draining my lizard on black jagged toilet stains. Sometimes a piece breaks off to reveal smoky white porcelain below. I think of things to tell people I dislike. You are a corpse draped in unshared insecurities. You are the culmination of weeknight parties and cruelty. If god did exist, he would laugh at you.

He tells me I hit a cat's head while on an entrance ramp. I start to cry until he tells me the cat was already dead and I just flattened the last bit, the head. I stop crying and wash off my tires when I get home. I'm starting to think people don't like her. Do my paintings create false representations of the human portrait?

Two dogs sit in the back of a truck on the interstate. One huddles close to the bed while the other presses his nose into the wind above the sedans passing by. He is unaware of the semi his owner is about to pass. He is ignorantly fixed on the sky and clouds and distant mountains. He is bliss. His hair tousles but he never blinks.

I hear noises through the bathroom door.

Concerned voices echo above the running shower and I think I'm being robbed. Then the music starts, a shredding guitar solo. I'm trying to stand up with the confidence of New York streets and tattoos but I shuffle around with rocks in my pockets waiting for floods. I leave the toilet seats up and look into bedrooms, longing.

She saw the Fleshlight on the drying rack and thought, "it was either you or me"
Alex Wilson

When we first met I promised myself I wouldn't lose my footing. But like military weaponry or pharmaceutical companies or language, things progressed regardless of my opinions.

Very little separates cathartic release from self-pity. How am I unlike the out of shape forty-something fawning over genetically superior millionaires playing games with the same seriousness as I treat my friends' deaths or girls who don't like me back?

A Wiccan alter sits below a drawing of the Pope being dragged to hell. People stop using my bathroom in fear all my Satanist jokes are real and avoiding my toilet will spare them from my inevitable decline into serial murder and human flesh consumption. I chew on the tip of my finger to get a taste.

They freeze my blood in blocks and shave it into flakes to float down onto the city below. When it rains blood, the apocalypse is starting. When it snows blood, children catch holiday themed misery on their tongues.

A man stands on the corner with thousands of

eyes instead of skin. Every time he blinks, someone dies. I wonder if he's looking at me. I wonder where he buys sunglasses. I wonder if my apartment would flood if he started to cry.

The concrete cracked my head open and, bit-by-bit, parts of me disappear into the storm drain. The key to perception is framing.

Trash Piles Up Around Me But My Mind's Never Been Clearer
Alex Wilson

I'm paying someone to deliver cookies. I don't have the ingredients for pancakes. Everyone's either drunk or stoned or tripping or out of their mind on deep contemplation, so no regular cake, and, besides, I don't trust them with frosting on my carpet.

Two people are exploring holes with different degrees of successful intimacy in the first bathroom. Someone's puking in the other. Some guy, in that half serious way so he can say he was just joking, tries to slip things into people's drinks.

A coked up gallery owner encourages us to fight in the middle of his Clive Barker exhibit entitled Tortured Cocks. His dog pisses on an original piece and he says he'll fix it tomorrow. The old church he lives in has balconies instead of bedrooms.

I'm flying over Nevada and the clouds billow into a frozen tundra. I wonder if polar bears and penguin can live in peace here or still need a world to separate them. I wonder if this is where Coke films its holiday commercials. There's a calming effect when you realize, at least for this moment, your life isn't in your hands.

My dad tells me he's uncomfortable in the middle of a record store, in the middle of a metal radio event, in the middle of people who don't care whether or not he fits their scene. I tell him that's how I feel in our hometown.

There's a knock at the door and I think the cookies are here.

I Only have a Few Minutes
Alex Wilson

Gordon had bashed open the window of my fourteenth floor apartment and climbed out onto the edge, gripping the broken glass that jetted out from the framing. Blood ran down the shards and dripped onto the hardwood floor of my apartment and I wondered how much longer I could stay awake.

Mandy and I kept our distance, trying not to spook Gordon as he peered over his shoulder to make sure we weren't getting too close. He had warned us if we took a step near him he would jump. At first we ran through the suicide talk we'd all seen on TV and in movies, all the cliché you have so much to live for bullshit. I now hoped we'd get to actual conversation.

"Did you really have to smash my window, man?" I asked. "It's a sliding fucking window. You could have just opened it."

"Don't you see the poetry in it?" asked Gordon. "The windows broken. I'm broken. Sort of like ethereal justice."

"That's the stupidest fucking thing I've ever heard."

"Can you have a bit more of a constructive attitude?" asked Mandy in a bitter tone.

70

Her Mohawk flopped to one side, dirty from two days of moving from bar to bar and not showering, only the sweat from each of our bodies to clean the other. Most of the time Mandy looked like the type of girl who would carry a box cutter but now her makeup ran down her cheeks in black tears.

The first time I saw Mandy she sat atop some tubby JC Penny suit wearing motherfucker's chest and, with some shiny brass knuckles, broke his fat baby face.

"The key to brass knuckles," she had said in between raking the guys molars out of his jaw, "is the swipe instead of punch head on. If you throw a fist like normal then you'll break your own hand."

A few teeth had fallen onto the concrete.

"You swing almost like a pendulum stroke."

When she had finished she had looked up at me, the city lights bouncing off the dumpster in the back of the dive bar.

"Rapists, man," she had laughed. "Everyone now a days thinks they have what it takes."

But now, the punk rock fuck you attitude I loved in her dissolved into the base reality of who we all were, scared clueless children fumbling for answers and validation.

"He's not suicidal," I told Mandy. "You're not

suicidal, are you man?" I said to Gordon.

"I'm standing on a fucking ledge. I'm not sure how much clearer I could be about my intent."

"Yeah, but if you were serious, you'd have jumped already. You just want us to listen to what you have to say or something. That's how these things work, right?" I reasoned.

"Maybe I just want you to hear a confession before I jump to my death, give an oral suicide note."

"Hey Chuck," started Mandy. "Shut the series fuck up. Are you trying to convince him to jump or some shit?"

"Don't get shitty with me. I'm fucking tired. I haven't been sober in days. I'm still not fucking sober. I'm hard and can't do shit about it."

"That's all you think about, yourself and my pussy."

Gordon turned towards us a bit more. His body wobbled for a moment but he gripped the broken glass on the framing tighter and regained his balance.

"You guys are going to fight now, at this moment, in this place? This is my suicide so can we focus on me?"

"Fine, Gordon," I blustered. "We'll talk about the

emotional baby who thinks this stunt is the best way to get a point across. Jesus, Gordon. Do we, do I really have to explicitly say please don't kill yourself for you to know I fucking care, to know I don't want you to be dead?"

"This isn't about you, Chuck," Gordon said.

"Then what the fuck is this about? Did Lana leave you? Is it about some ex-girlfriend? Some mommy and daddy issue? Did you not get a letter back from Mr. Rodgers as a kid?"

"It's not about any of that!" yelled Gordon.

His feet shifted against the blurry backdrop. The shards beneath him caught the Chicago city lights and my eyes ran along the windowsill littered with fragments of glass.

"How did you break the window?" I asked.

"What?" responded Gordon.

"How did you break my fucking window? What did you smash it with?"

"I found a baseball bat in your bedroom."

"The baseball bat hung up over my bed?"

"Yeah."

"The one in the glass case?"

73

"Yeah, Chuck."

"The one signed by the Cubs?"

"I don't know who the fuck signed it."

I took a step closer to Gordon, my eyes bleeding dry of sympathy to be replaced with an anger blind to situational circumstance.
"The one my dad gave me just before he died?"

Gordon said nothing, his eyes darting between the shattered glass fragments at the edge of his life and my rage.

"And where is it now?"

"I lost my grip when I swung, it feel." He looked down to the street."Fucking jump."

"Don't you dare let go!" pounded Mandy.

"If you don't jump then I'm throwing you out the fucking window. Go kill yourself. Say what ever you need to say then just step out into the air."

Mandy turned her gaze to me once again, a distraction or a devil she hated for a moment but would then forget.

"It's a god damn baseball bat, Chuck. If he dies because of you then I'm bashing in your skull."

I ignored Mandy and thought about my father,

long dead, who had given me the baseball bat. When I was younger he would brandish it at me, as if he would strike me with it for my misbehaviors. He never did but that was mentality of my father, to put on a show without a bang.

Mandy peered at my blank stare of remembrance then turned her attention to Gordon who's eyes also fixed at my pondering.

"Gordon, you have our attention. If you have something to say then say it. Just ignore Chuck." Mandy's words took me back into the moment and my anger mixed with a longing sadness. Now I was drunk, high, horny, confused, upset, furious, and I bereaved.

Gordon's eyes glassed over and his pupils rose towards the ceiling, peering over our heads and looking off into a distance that didn't exist. I found myself uninterested and still lacking sympathy for a friend in crisis.

"When you're a kid you have this crazy interest in the world around you but then you start school and all those questions you have become burdens to people too tired to provide answers. You get all these ideas about changing the world and breaking the monotony of your parents, of everyone you've ever encountered. You tell yourself those dreams you have will fulfill themselves with hard work then life starts to catch up. You need to pay rent, keep a gym membership, drink enough to forget all the responsibly. Then you get married, have a kid, you have this person to look after, questions to be burdened by. All those little joys warp into responsibilities, routines, places to fill voids. You get old and everyone you know starts to die. Standing at grave sites, you can't help but wonder what your life will mean. Suddenly some nurse who's life you've lived ten times over is wiping your ass and you're just dying alone."

"Stop fucking whining," I snapped. "Boo hoo, you have the exact same problem as everyone else in the world and you can't deal because you aren't special and unique enough. You relate too much to the rest of us fucking mouth breathers."

"You know, you're a bastard," said Gordon. "I'm about the jump to my death and you're giving me shit."

"You're jumping for no other reason than you're growing up."

"Lana's pregnant," cut in Mandy. "She's pregnant, isn't she?"

I turned to her, confused by how she came to the conclusion. From the corner of my eye I noticed Gordon had also turned to look at her.

"Yeah," said Gordon. "How'd you know?"

"Nothing makes you grow up quicker than a

broken rubber," said Mandy, triumphant. "And Gordon, if you jump out the window and splatter on the ground I'll make sure that kid grows up knowing their father was a coward, too afraid to even meet them. I'll make the brat resent you more than anyone. Your legacy will be the fading memory of a fear filled man who gave up because he created life."

"Harsh," I whispered.

"If there's one thing you've been trying to say tonight, it's that life's harsh," demanded Mandy, not breaking gaze with Gordon.

My eyes jumped between them both, deer in headlights, just waiting for the car to hit. Gordon's knees started bend as he kneeled down. His right foot stepped off the window's edge and onto the sill but the blood running down from his hand hadn't dried and he slipped, falling backwards out the window.

Mandy and I both looked at each other for a moment before inching over to the window, to see our friend as a red splotch on a far away sidewalk and street. I wondered if Mandy would still tell Gordon's offspring he was a coward for accidently killing himself. Maybe she'd just describe him as clumsy. I hoped my bat had by luck fallen in a sparse city bush and remained relatively intact.

As my feel slid closer to the gaping night air I started to hear a muffled panic. When Mandy and I looked over the edge we saw Gordon gripping the concrete architecture, his legs flailing over the city.

"You're like the kid too scared to jump off the diving board at the local swimming pool but slips and falls in when he tries to get down," I joked.

"Pull me the fuck up!" screamed Gordon.

"I'll go grab my baseball bat. I think it's long enough to reach you."

"Fuck you!"

"Fucking Christ, Gordon," shouted Mandy. "Let me look around, see if there's anything that can reach you."

Mandy scurried through my apartment, pulling drawers opened, tying sheets together and checking their strength, trying to find anything we could pull Gordon up with.

"I'm sorry about the baseball bat," said Gordon.

"Yeah, you should be."

Mandy came back with the towel bar from my bathroom. With all the adrenalin pumping through her body she had ripped the screwed-in rack right out of my bathroom, chunks of dry wall still clinging to the edges. She leaned over the broken window and I grabbed her hips so she wouldn't fall too. Gordon took the bar with one hand then transferred all his hopes to live onto something designed to hold the weight of a wet towel. Mandy and I both pulled and Gordon reached the window once more.

We all leaned against the wall, the broken window above us, the howling winds of Chicago sending chills our minds now noticed through the apartment, broken glass digging through our pants and poking our skin. We passed a cigarette between the three of us.

"When I fell all I could think about was regretting ever stepping close to the edge."

"Was falling to your death in real life like falling in a dream, same sensation?" I passed the cigarette to Gordon.

"Sort of," said Gordon, taking a drag. "Though, when the peril is real everything moves in slow motion, maybe my thoughts just came faster."

Gordon passed the cigarette to Mandy.

"Do you guys think an angel watched over us tonight, like we had a godly experience?" asked Gordon.

"I think all those demon and angel stories are bullshit. We're the ones who save each other, same goes for tempting," I said, watching Mandy ash out the last ember by dragging the cigarette across the bottom of her shoe.

"You're saying we're our own demons and saviors?" asked Mandy.

I stood up and walked towards my bedroom.

"I'm saying maybe we're all just fuck heads making the whole thing up as we go."

Alien

Emily Black

I open my eyes

and to the world

you've dropped dead. The grass

grew green here all my life

until it started sprouting black.

It's like I fall

to slumber each night with my head in

a fishbowl helmet of whiskey; waking

to stumble each morning on

outlandish terrain. Where am I?

Where are you? Where to plant my feet, the flag?

Existence is alien without your lover.

I find the ground turns purple and blue like you do.

The atmosphere I'm intaking makes me choke

up. My brain stays the same

here, wherever, and I've still

got questions for your answers: I'll just

hurl them to the sky hoping they catch

you on the tail-end of a cascading comet,

I guess.

Am I your seething heart's

crater hole too, honey? The wonder can

blister you alive, I know. It's everything we used

to have, before it went sour, got broader.

Did you recite the stars' order wrong? When you
thought

the fellow in the constellation was jutting a hitchhiker's
thumb,

and he just meant to say you're doing it right;

stay. And

are you in a tailspin, on your hastily returning getaway
shuttle,

as you jet steady back to the world a bang built;

rebuilt each time we met

gazes: Bang, Bang, Bang.

Some day I'll care

for travelling—going real far.

When the concentration of

everyone who sustains me isn't

knit up in our hometown

homecoming scarf's colors. I never wanted to be

anywhere you aren't. Not down

the street, in exotic landscapes, on

this planet or any other. I think when

the day ends and takes my life

with it, I just hoped you felt how I did. If

So be a leader,

pick up your phone. Take me back, take me

home.

Collapse
Emily Black

A house stands strong and stable as

a government, and nothing

more. Both can become a tough wind's

victims. The streets pay when that happens.

They crawl in those without law

or living room, suddenly speckled in sticky

coins;

the confetti of celebrations for capitalism with a

capital C. But here they're just

breadcrumbs, and everyone's

starving.

A man wears pants—and only that—

from the days when war was work but at least

there was work; Enough! Enough! Enough!

as the chants say.

The wages made a home, and the home made him

human. But he was on the wrong end of enough and

eventually came the collapse; where

shelter went to the wolves and people went only one

way: up or down. He fell

alongside everything else.

This time a crowd gathers on the corner, and gather

him in their arms in a bundle. It's

funny, he thinks, through eyesight that's already

seen its last scrap of humor,

for them to care because they did

not yesterday, and in the tomorrow that delivers

their birthright's snarling Bentleys everyone will find
it's

much the same.

To the Long Nights
Emily Black

Panic pursues a bell's toll. In the youngest

days it seemed that time became too late

with a bold black smudge; blotting and stark

on white daylight. Clock's two handles angled
heavenward:

dubbed midnight but the very latest limit allowed

as a kid for open eyes and roving legs. The hour struck
—

hard, and your pillowset had better be the next

stop on the day's docket for its rest. To sleep we'd go

like soldiers.

The more turns the world took it dawned on me

that sacrificing a sunset is sacrilege. Slumber while your
watch

still shone in single digits spits at everything

that's nocturnal and natural. I don't want to retire too
early;

as adolescents we retired the term curfew and

bargained

with one another: stay awake instead. From there and then

we found truth and trouble, and for the littlest hours

paid full price.

In the dark the danger sits surface-level.

The most madcap of questions come,

shaped by the damp portals of mouths lifting

from beer bottles, wheat-whispering:

What's your ultimate fantasy? Clink against

the teeth, slink in your eye. I tell you I won't tell you,

and in your jilted rattle and hissing about it you're missing

that that's just because you've already made it

so. Little me had vivid dreams

where there were fields not yet drenched

in dew. Lying upon the grass without blankets

as barriers, angled elbows and open-palm pillows

making for the position for

87

surveying stars with precision. They stay

mostly stationary but we shoot our indexing fingers

at them anyway, making asteroids of glowing fish-white

skin in the dark. Yes it's a reverie where we reside in reality.

You might call it, plain and presumably joked, tonight.

Say yes to the long night. You don't belong

to your bed until the last of the lamplight winks,

the lively light extinguished in each

friends' face. You could have hours left over

to be together. The show reels its credits, the pizzabox centerpiece;

this evening's masterpiece, offers now only ghosts as grease.

Don't let that dictate a goodbye and scatter

for homebase. It's midnight. Who's got another idea? Toss the keys.

Cover the clock.

As long as I'm awake the drumbeat of my dreams

have their best chance at seeing light—and

it might just be the morning's.

New Age Ruckus
Austin Farrell

Uncanny faces
Fruity vapor
Jazzy weeknight
8-Bit Pale Ale

Tin shed
    Tattered sofa
Rat-a-tat snares
Big Muff chords
    Bass line thunder
Oscillating spines

    Sparkling sidewalks
Rubberneckers
Backspacers
    Intersubjectivity

Cool Kids

Austin Farrell

Bass lines billow smoothly under
cheap earbuds' rattle static fuzz
as he lurks down sidewalks,
haunting bystanders through dark shades
while murmuring some lyrics from
The King of Carrot Flowers,
the song that played when
he strutted from Sociology class
to the hookah lounge with
Brenton, John, and other goons,
discussing the trouble they'll cause
where white, dim streetlights flicker
on their shiny grins while
handing over a sandwich bag
filled with dried, natural wonders
that will make anyone go
right out their front door
and into the saturated evening,
purple, and orange fused clouds
against abnormal apartment complex geometry,
breezes that excite nervous systems,

and it never felt better
except when they were younger,
smiling at every little thing
that their eyes freely scanned,
not knowing how to frown
until the first real crush
walked away with someone else,
but they got over it,

trudging through high school halls
into university labyrnths with strangers,
becoming the goons that would
be shoved into jail cells
for being merry pranksters and
obeying their visions of harmony.

A Few Words for Jalen
Austin Farrell

When we put it on our tongues
waiting for the carpet to spiral,
when our faces became heavy
and slowly turned smiles out,

When we stepped out on the balcony
watching trees breathe and dance,
when we saw a grown hipster couple
holding hands and grocery bags,

When we rode in the back of my Silverado
driven by a good friend and madness,
when we waited for the starter to kick
like the beginning of a rollercoaster ride,

When we rode through heated districts
while manufactured families loitered,
when we glided by them slowly
with their sharp eyebrows and warped mouths,

When we stepped inside Little Bread
and met Jacob at the isolated table,
when we talked about dropping out
and living through pen strokes,

When we met up with Maddie
pointing out the trees that mattered,
when we walked through Wilson Park
watching first kiss and picnic clichés manifest,

When we went to have coffee

as our bodies got used to gravity again,
when we began to realize nature
reeked of cement and rotting wood,

When we finally split up and retired
to our temporary homes for the evening,
When I got back and parked my truck,
I really just wanted to keep driving.

Leave, Stay, Go

Faith Hoatson

First you leave,
You don't know why you're leaving.
Your body feels suspended, as a mere vessel for
thought.

But here you are, already out the door.

You stay, until you realize
until your heart pounds at the wall of your chest
You stay until
you feel stuck.

Then, you cannot wait to go. You will
not
feel happy,
contented,
fulfilled
until your feet are planted in this mystified *elsewhere.*

Now you have left again,
and you do not quite know why you're leaving.

You fade in and out of the stories
She knew me once…He knew me then.
You are person they intersect with,
and then hurry on towards their destinations.

But still, you go.

You leave their lives, and become their memories
You go,
you seek the stories of elsewhere.

No Answer Keys, please.

Faith Hoatson

Take up that profession which will secure
a 9-5 pace, an endless race to the weekend.

Buy textbooks with answer keys, for classes
vested in rigid answers and concrete developments

Take solace in the phrase "I'm right. You're wrong."
Monotony can feel like home,
just as domestically-pleasing as a toilet cleaning.

Wake up, and have a revelation.
Stare down the plumbing, mulling the excrement over.

Rip the answer keys from your books,
Refuse to only wonder what is meant to be wondered

Break off, start a new beat, and grab that worn
paperback at your bedside instead.

Nomads
Faith Hoatson

It makes sense that people were once nomadic.

It is our natural inclination
the seemingly intrinsic tendency
to wander, to wonder, to seek freedom

Perhaps that's why there are so many starving artists
and a cultural abhorrence for the one-percent

At the heart of humanity
beats the nomad,
the homeless
unsure of where his next meal will come
but certain that each dawn carries new challenges

Nomads, aren't we all? Ever-fighting, ever-shifting
Dynamic – electric- souls

Eager, yet hesitant, for each sunrise
As the sunset is a final bliss before rest,
a sunrise is a restless heart beating once again.

I for Ignorance

Mina Apostadiro

I was blinded --
it surrenders itself
enslaved
to the wind that pulls at its heels
and the words it carries to your grave
(how brave).
The collapse,
of the duality in a corrupt Blessing
and a holy Sin
If it cries in heaven but sings in hell
would that make you its kin?
House me,
(what a natural occurrence)
and fill in my void with Home.
There's an innocence to the absence
of yours
(when does it happen?)
You're among them
bodies of
nomadic roaming.
Souls you hardly scratch
are merely an attack
on what lies beneath
the earth's skin.
The Twin Flames
reflect back

gray, cold ashes
of your unresolved,
projected
shadow.
It gnaws at your strings
flooding with sorrow
whispering permission
anticipating a moment
of weakness.
Attempts are fostered,
and confused,
fragmented,
lust
returns with a commission
-- soon after ignorance began to blossom.

Secrets

Mina Apostadiro

Ribbons of gray
and ash blue
dance slowly before my eyes
How lovely and heartbreaking,
I thought,
would it be to embody a streak of the sky's
endless hues?
It would be lovely
to halt lives and hold a gaze
for more than a few seconds by my soft shade alone.
But reality bleeds farther
than that of wishful thinking.
I am only but
a whisper
in a sky full of screams.
How
does one compare?

Sober Reality
Mina Apostadiro

She loves to drink with the memories of her past,
Shots of broken promises,
And feelings that should have last.
She takes swigs of her favorite retentions,
All which embrace him.
She lets its ambiguous liquid take over,
As her mind begins to spin.
She sips on their 'first times', his smile,
And the secrets she told.
But feels thoughtless for defining one name as
'everything',
And for losing her hold.

She now slurs every thought,
And clouds every decision.
Because life was once satiated of value,
And clear with precision.

She's an alcoholic, you see?
Drunk off of the idea of happily ever after,
And sweet serendipity.

They tell her to "move on,
To let go, and forget."
But she is intoxicated with one part nostalgia,

And two parts regret.

She longs for the day,
When he returns home.
Because if it is there in her past,
Where she can find him,
She'll stay and have a drink.

Intrinsic Paintings
Mina Apostadiro

Come dressed or entirely undressed, of the experiences that clothe the skin of your curves. In all of the time I've grown to know you, you have not looked more beautiful than you lay, fast asleep, right now. Appear strong or completely vulnerable, of the abstract thoughts that drown your mind. I see it in your habits whose pains have become too comfortable -- as to why I secure my fingers only that much tighter when I feel the tremble of yours. Express yourself through the roar of the ocean's chaotic release, or remain silent like the froth that skips along its shore. Your presence and the impact of its touch is the work of a miraculous being -- however to get you to realize your light is a miracle all on its own. But that isn't stopping me. Dance in the errors or corrected misspellings of the world's suggestions and all of the feelings they leave you with. Because above all, I want you to come as you are. Come as all and any matters of the desires you stand and wish to be. I indulge in the knowledge of everything I hold and have yet to grasp about you. And I realize such thing is an absolute gift. Although the horizons both behind and before us blur life with zealous uncertainty, I wish to serve as the same beauty as you do in mine. Because while change thrives as the only constant in life, I don't seek to alter your print with the hand of an artist who isn't you -- for I realize that

love sings beyond the words of acceptance and beauty,
which no way entails changing the soul of a person to
match a preference.

Phobic Solitude

Mina Apostadiro

You try to savagely uproot the cause of every situation played as problematic in the hopes you'd find something beautiful that stemmed out of complete and utter hideousness. But you don't. The movies pictured on screens only cause you to falsely hope for answers that make sense in a dirt that shouldn't. And it doesn't. Because as you carry the secret of a loss of innocence and a loss of trust for the flowers that bloom before your eyes, you understand that not everyone hums it in the same melody as you do. Nevertheless, it still plants itself into every aspect of your life. And it's okay. It is completely and entirely okay. She, too, bleeds the same color as he does. You and I share the same hue of crimson beneath our skin. But the difference lies beneath the preference that grows within each bud that blossoms the decision you keep hidden away. Stop hiding. Because although we are bred into a society who has yet to throw the wilted leaves of ignorance away, do not ever feel for a second that you have to cut the roots of everything that once kept you grounded.

A Three Minute Essay
Emily Talapa

She says her arms burn when she's shoveling snow. But she likes it because she hopes that the warmth from her arms will help melt the snow. Then she won't have as much to shovel. It warms her. It's nighttime.

She says sometimes when she's alone she'll listen to songs that are rich in strings, that build gradually. She moves in slow motion like she's in a film. She tells me she has twelve hundred followers on Instagram but doesn't even know a hundred people. She says she wants to leave the island of thigh gaps and bra straps and filters. Wants to go to an island where these things aren't things. There will be jade plants there that sit in windowsills and rain that is warm sometimes if you choose to run in it. White chocolate is sold in ribbons and a full night's rest is simple. Dogs snore on porches and the sun comes when it isn't raining.

She's rereading The Hobbit but upside down this time so it lasts longer. She pictures her face on Bilbo's body. She was Bilbo once. It makes her think about how she was Bilbo once.

When she cries her tears taste like pistachio gelato. They collect on her lips. Then she's walking in Florence again at night and she's holding her tears in a cone in her fist. They drip on her wrist. Green. Light green.

She says she often dreams about running for trains in a Munich station — München Hauptbahnhof. They're enormous and they hiss and they puff out smoke. She sees one that says, "Your Dreams." She starts to run towards it. It's leaving the station. As she's running she sees one that says, "Your Future." She wonders why they are separate trains. She turns to run for "Your Future" and realizes that it's not what she wants. Deciding against it, she turns once more to the other train. It's pulling away. Quickly. Her legs are pumping. She doesn't know if she will make it.

She tells me that she kicks so hard in her sleep that she wakes herself up. All of her pillows are off of her bed and it's three in the morning. She can't sleep so she walks downstairs to make hot ginger tea. Watches the snow fall. Thinks about shoveling.

Bilbo is in the window of one of the trains but she can't ever remember which train he's sitting in. "I could make a guess," she says. But she doesn't know for sure. She hopes he is in a certain train.

She says she's in the shower now and her arms burn from brushing her hair. It's okay though because the water is cold. It's running cold.

Dominicana
Josh Carr

The room was dimly lit by the morning sun filtering through the half drawn blinds. The tropic heat was almost unbearable in the late spring and, though the room was mostly draped in shadows and the day was still very young, the humidity of the room was growing unbearable. The sound of a child's laugh drifted in on the warm wind, and it was enough to jolt me from my bed. I sat on the edge of my bunk and looked around the room. It looked much more like a barracks than what many would expect to find in the city. Rows of bunks were arranged along the thirty-some-odd foot wall, their ends jutting out into the room. Along the opposite wall, there were three more bunks arranged parallel to the wall and to their right were two doors. Two windows were the only things that graced the otherwise pale white walls. One was situated next to my bunk. I stood and looked out the window, peering through the bars to see as much un-obscured scenery as I could. Across the alley there was a child playing on a multi-colored plastic side. Not much about that fact was particularly odd, aside from the fact that it was on the roof the adjacent building. *That's not something you see back home,* I thought to myself. It's a saying I had thought quite frequently since arriving in Santo Domingo the day before.

I washed up, dressed and headed down to the dining room. The kitchen was no larger than one that could be found in any American household, rather decidedly smaller. The cooks that staffed the small kitchen where locals, and volunteers from the parish a few blocks down the street. It was the sister parish to the South Gorham Baptist Church, where the team was based out of. Eggs and toast with a glass of water and I was ready for the day. I have to admit, as foreign as the spices seemed at time, it was comforting to start the day with a home cooked meal; even if it wasn't from my own home.

That small comfort was something I truly needed, as at this point every other part of the day was spent thousands of miles outside of my comfort zone. Being in a urban environment was foreign enough. A small town kid from rural Maine was a strange traveler to the the landscape of towering high rises and decaying slums. This, ofcourse, was not the most foreign element of my temporary residence. That city was so unlike the cities I had encountered in the States. Boston, Orlando, Las Vegas; they were nothing compared the the sights, sounds and smells of La Romana. In downtown Las Vegas, you don't really see many gas station attendants with Spas-12's or men guarding DMV's with M-16s. Well, at least you don't see it in public. Regardless, there was an air of lawlessness that hung over the city that is absent in the U.S. Years of strife and struggle and a handful of military coups have left the country in an unstable political climate. The military and the police are not always separate entities, and behind the curtain of a simple, albeit difficult life, lie elements of tension and xenophobia. That was the third world, and the rules there were different. It was a set of rules this young adventurer was not used to.

All and all, it was still a very beautiful place. The mountains to the north provided a distant backdrop of extensive green jungle, pockmarked with tiny villages along the slopes that led down into valleys of sprawling green sugar cane. The villages themselves were a sight to behold for reasons all their own. I had a chance to visit two of the villages while I was in the country. On the day after arriving in country, the entirety of the group, both the Medical and Construction team, traveled North of the city to a remote village nestled deep in a mass of cane fields. The rough dirt road that brought the rickety bus into the village was its only connection to the outside world. The dozen buildings that would pass as their homes were painted bright colors, faded by the sun and broken up with the occasional spray of mud. The tin roofs were a rusted red color, and seemed to be moments from collapsing. Clothes were displayed on drying lines, forming a faded rainbow along the sides of the partially crumbling buildings. On the far side of the small valley village, there was a clearing that had been cut away from the surrounding cane and flattened to make a miniature baseball field. Slick muddy trails made up the base line, each leading to a patch of dried mud, wider than the trails, that acted as a base. As the medical team ran a brief clinic, the construction team, of which I was a member, played a game of baseball with a new baseball brought for the children and a bat one of the residents had hand carved from the branch of a tree with an old cane machete.

The second village was completely different. Four days into the trip, the Medical team brought some of the construction crew on to help with a much larger clinic in one of the more populated villages. The setup and sights were similar to the last. However the village was spread out over a few densely packed acres, with only

111

one public bathroom to serve the community. The clinic ran for most of the day yet, of the dozens of people that passed through the doors of the small mountain church, only one patient caught my attention. Half way through the day, a young child walked through the double doors and wandered from station to station. His teeth were cleaned, and after the doctors had examined him, he made his way to my station, a baggie of medication in hand. It was only then that I realized why I had fixated on the child, who couldn't have been more than eight years old. He was alone. He had no adult with him. It was his bravery that had struck me. The boy didn't shed a tear or so much as hesitate. It was more bravery than I had seen, even in adults. At eight years old, the young boy knew that he needed the care, and regardless of how terrifying it must have been to go to this clinic alone and subject himself to the care of foreigners whom he had never met, he faced it with his head held high. Meds in hand, and new clothes slung over his shoulder, the young boy headed out the rear door of the church, looking back for only a moment with a slight smile as he surveyed the room one last time. With that, he turned back and disappeared into the mass of people in the muddy street just beyond the doorway.

* * *

I heaved another bag of cement onto my shoulders, and carried it to the second floor of the job site. From the half finished room, a foreman yelled.

"Necesitamos más bloques!"

"We need another round of blocks up here," said

our translator. "Tell the rest of the crew."

I sighed, wiping the sweat from my forehead with a bandana. "Ok," I replied before turning around and jogging back down the stairs. "Mierda," I cursed under my breath as the sharp coral-laced cinder blocks cut deeply into my hands. I had taken to using spanish whenever I dared to curse, though it was always too quiet to be heard. It was a church trip after all, but I was among the only three members that spoke any spanish. The chances I would been heard were small, and the chances of being understood were far smaller. The pain, however, got to me from time to time. My gloves had long since been shredded and I refused to take anyone else's.
"No sense in both of us getting torn up," I responded, attempting to be cheerful.

The sun beat down on the crew and the wind kicked up the dust from the dirt road that ran through the fevella. The small shanty town was in far worse shape than the mountain villages. The homes were either made of crumbling cement or of tin sheeting; more often being a strange mixture of the two. Standing on the half-built second floor of what would one day be a school, you could see for about mile in any direction, all of which was just more of the same. Shanty after shanty, shack after shack, each seemingly more decrepit than the rest. The few spaces that were left of open field, where the children would often play, were strewn with a collage of plastic bags, food wrappers and a vast array of cardboard boxes. Each one, a relic of a rare trip to Jumbo or a local bodega. Each bag, that once was a carrier of hope, now passively opposed the progress it had furthered.

In the middle of the dirt driveway next to the work site, a small child had been playing most of the day. As I threw himself to the dirt and reached for a water, enjoying one of the few breaks the crew was rarely afforded, I finally took a moment to actually observe what the child was doing. He was lost in his own world, using his toy truck to pretend to help the workers. He would load up the cut out section of the milk carton, which made the body and bed of the truck, with bits of coral and gravel and tow the truck around with a string. Load after load, the small Pringle-lid wheels turned on their pencil axles, carrying the gravel to the other end of the driveway. The boy had the biggest grin on his face as he carted his mini payload around. He was a hard worker, for only four years old and derived a great joy from helping the crew.

Of all the sights I experienced on the trip, the one that would stick with him for years was the simplest. The smiles. The smile of the young boys as they faced overwhelming poverty. The smiles of the cooks, always happy to help and fiercely proud of their cooking, as they should be. The smiles of the men and women of the fevella as they worked every day to not live, but survive. They lived in one room shanties, no larger than an American living room and fed their extended families on dollars a day. Yet every day, they would greet you with a warm smile and a genuine conversation. They were happy to see you, even if they didn't know you. They asked for nothing, and worked for everything they had. At the end of the day, they attended church and went home with their families, proud. Not the vain pride that plagues our nation, but the simple pride of a father or mother who was able to provide for their family.

Later that evening, as the plates in the dining room were cleared away and the warm tropical air began to cool, I sat down with a pen and pad to write with one question looming in my mind: Why did I have to travel to the third world, to learn how to live in my own?

Under The Pines
Josh Carr

I sat under a tall pine tree, shaded from where the light touches. With some effort I pulled myself to my feet, slung my Henry's over my shoulder, and brushed the leaves off of my blue woolen uniform. At this point, why did it matter? The blue fibers were stained permanently with the dark brown dirt tossed up by the cannon shells and the deep red of the blood, not all of it my own. Fall was upon the eastern forests, and even today it was a sight to see.

In the open field, just outside the tree line, the leaves burned the colors orange and yellow and consumed large swaths of land. Their consumption spread as their brothers fell, one by one, to the burning earth. The scene was a picture of glory; A picture worthy of one's memory.

From where I stood, back pressed against the tree as to keep to my feet, I could see a broader picture. The glory ceased where the sun refused to shine. What was once the great burning earth in the sunlight faded into shades of dull grey and brown, as the fallen leaves littered the ground. They seemed tired, worn down by the bitter cold and the violent winds. Their broken shells, once full of life and color, now deadened; crushed under the weight of battle and the boots of men. Darker still, under the cover of the great green conifers, lay a few of the same deadened leaves. Separated from their brothers and far from the field where the masses lay, they bore an even worse fate. Just as trampled, as tired and as broken, yet they face it alone under the shadows of the pines.

My feet had ceased to hold me, and I collapsed to the ground yet again. My rifle clattered across the tree's roots and landed a few feet away. It was no matter; I no longer needed it. The sharp pains in my gut and my thigh we slowly dulling, and shadows were growing darker. I lay there, quietly reflecting as I waited for my fate. My last breath out was a long one; one I knew would not come back to me. As the last of it left my chilled lungs, a brown leaf fell upon my outstretched hand. What cruel wind blew it here, to end its life in shadow? To end its life alone?

Season of Awakening

Amelia Weber

My kiss is the dawn.

When my lips caress the Earth,

she awakens.

The sun lights up her curves

as I trace along her hills and valleys.

She glows.

A breath of air escapes my lips,

ruffles through her hair.

The trees,

the grass,

all shiver and sway.

Her eyes open

sweeping up from her cheeks

like flowers exploding into bloom.

In her eyes are rippling pools of color

breaking free from the ice.

Never were they still as they remained frozen under
her eyelids.

Always the waves crash over them,

hidden thoughts never to be spoken.

Frozen overnight as she dreamt of tomorrow.

Tomorrow, when dawn would come

to wake her.

At the sight of me.

At the sight of dawn,

her core thaws.

A hushed sigh fill the air with warmth

as she turns towards the light

and away from the darkness of night.

No longer does she sleep alone in cold sheets.

I am here to warm her.

A smile spreads across her face,

a welcome sight in the gloom.

With full force I return to her shores,

carving a path of barren earth.

In my wake spread all of the warmth of life

as I watch her start to grow.

Trembling, shaking, fighting,

it struggles to reach the surface.

And at last,

new life is created,

bursting forth from within her.

Never has she been so beautiful

as in this moment.

I watch as my work

takes hold,

spreading to each cold, lonely space

until nothing is left but

her warmth,

her glow.

The sea of emotion

within her eyes

is now settled.

Calm are the waters,

just right for a dip.

A gentle hand, like a flock of birds

darts out before me.

She knows I will be leaving

I am no longer needed.

She is warm.

She is alive.

I am not needed
Until the day she is frozen once more

cold and alone and in need

of my kisses of the dawn.

A World With Happiness
Corey Yuman

"President Kanye West Re-Elected!"

Any newspaper that Marshall picks up on November 6th, 2024 was going to have that exact headline. He knew reading it would make him angry, yet he does it anyway. He glances over the article with the biggest thing sticking out to him being "re-election concert set for 7:00 PM, invite only" which makes him instantly crumple the paper and toss it to the ground.

"A damn concert to celebrate re-election? Fuck this world," Marshall mumbles to himself.

Marshall takes his beanie out of his pocket, putting it over his short hair.

"Sir, where am I?" A voice pops up behind Marshall.

As Marshall turns around he becomes taken aback by a young boy.
"Hell, kid." Marshall says to the boy. "But you look like you already know that."

The boy trembles ever so slightly by what Marshall says, so Marshall he tries to settle him down before he gets too upset.

"So, what's the name kid?" Marshall asks.

"Kenny," the boy replies.

"OK, hello Kenny. So why don't you know where you are?"

"Well, I'm from South Chi, and I was with..."

"Ahhh, so your parents are part of the Yeezus Party. We call you converted around these parts. You lost then or what?" Marshall interrupts. "Well, come on kid, you just going to stare at me or talk? Speak up,".

"My school bus left without me on the trip."
"Ahh lord, well I don't have any home, so if you're lookin for a roof you're lookin in the wrong place. Aren't you getting your free education?"

"Yeah, I'm in the advanced learning grades at the Church of Yeezus."

"Church of what? You know, I don't even care. All the free education in America isn't going to prepare you for the shit hole this place has become."

Marshall starts to walk away, but Kenny hurries to catch up.

"My Dad and Mom always say it was the homeless that was stopping the President from reaching his goals," Kenny mustered up the courage to say.

"Well they weren't lying to ya about that."

"So it wasn't a lie?"
"Nahh. It started with Trump getting elected. God damn kid, how old are you even?"
"12. Well, 12 next month," Kenny says having trouble keeping up with Marshall's speed.

"Ahh lord, so this world is all you know. Ok, it's like this. President Trump was elected, people fled to whatever country would let them in. President West gets elected because people misconceived him as some sort of rap God, even more dip out. But some of us stayed. Over the course of the last eight years the last two Presidents have flipped America into a fucking punchline. It's all turned into a giant playground for them."

"Should I be remembering this? Or even getting what you're talking about?"

"Come on kid, you really trying to tell me that you're in some sort of advanced class but can't even keep up with recent history? It isn't like I'm asking you to explain the history of battle rap to me or some shit."

Kenny stares back blankly as Marshall realizes that any more explaining isn't going to get him anywhere.

"So what do ya know?"

"Mom always says it's cuz of President Kanye that there's free school, and people don't die over money because he got rid of it and...."

Marshal quickly cuts him off. "Yeah, yeah, yeah. I know all about what your parents are going to have said. People are just happy because they get their little toys free now. Do we really need mandatory iPhones? Anything shiny to distract a person. Any book to read for class that will make them feel smarter, because that false sense of superiority can be an addictive high. That's why those of that didn't run away are dangerous. We just need the cause."

"Why stay just to not have a home?" Kenny stopped.

"To fight for what once was. To be engulfed in what's going on. You can't change anything by moving to England, or sitting on your couch."

"Just seems weird."

"Get your scriptures! Get your scriptures!" The sound of the robotic newspaper stands making its trip around the block.

"Weird? That's the thing kid. That robot over there doesn't seem weird to you. The president releasing a daily journal that are just his tweets called *The Scripture* doesn't seem weird to you. Ration centers that decide how much food you get, every six months the Pledge of Allegiance being different lyrics of his songs, and Government employees being called Yeezus Disciples are just usual to you. That's what's weird. How everything can change so fuckin quick.."

 Frustrated, Marshall walks faster. A few moments pass Kenny starts running after him.

"Sir, sir!" The kid yells, catching up. "What's your name?"

"Marshall. Now why don't you just get lost kid?"

"I AM lost! I need to find my way to Mercy Park for President Kanye's re-election concert. I didn't get back on my school bus in time and they left without me!"

Marshall stops in his tracks.

"You kidding me? You have a invite? Why didn't you

just say so. I'll get you there. It's a bit of a walk, " The two make a sudden left, Marshall reaches for his bag and sifts through it looking for something to keep Kenny occupied. "Here, eat an apple."

The pace speeds up, as Marshall's heart starts beating fast. The President rarely makes a public appearance a year and a half since the last time to be exact. Most wondered how he was re-elected but a string of new music made to express his re-election goals and promises caught on like no campaign ever before.

About two hours pass. After tossing Kenny on his back the two picked up steam. As they approached the gate to get into the park Marshall sets Kenny down.

"Ok, now give me the ticket, just follow what I say so I can get you back to your group. I don't wanna be in this place any longer than I have to be. I'm gonna call you my son to get in, just to make sure you're safe."

They have the Ticket Disciple in sight. He was just a teenage kid. His Mom or Dad likely with a Government job so they assigned him this looking to get his foot in the door.

"Hey, my son got separated from his school group. I picked him up, and got him here as soon as I could. Could I just take him in there really quick? Here's his pass," Marshall says showing him.

"Yeah, whatever, just hurry out before someone wants your pass too," the Disciple says. Marshall thinks about how that kid's future in Government is done once people found out who they let in, but brushes it out of his mind quickly and gets back to the mission.

They walk into the park grounds, looking at the mass of people. Before Marshall can even look at the ticket to try to find a seat section Kenny yells, "Mrs. Hazelton!"

The teacher turns, seeing Kenny. Her face turning beet red as she looks around at the children, just then noticing he was not on the bus.

"Thanks Marshall!" Ken yells from back in his group, and is suddenly getting scolded by the teacher as they march off.

Marshall grabs the inside of his pocket, feeling the Beretta he always carries for the one in a trillion chance he would have everything fall together like this.

He looks at the stage, seeing the flashing lights flicker over everyone's face. If you focused on one person their face would run the gauntlet of colors from the strobe lights. An aura was in the air. An energy impalpable to everyone but Marshall for he knew in his heart what was about to come.

He starts to shove his way through the crowd. Slowly but surely his aggression is getting him closer. The crowd fully erupting in chants of "Yeezus" as the voice they've been waiting to hear took the stage.

"I've been waitin' on this my whole life. These dreams be wakin' me up at night," President Kanye raps.

Marshall edges as close as he can. His aim has to be perfect.

"You say I think I'm never wrong, You know what,

maybe you're right...aight?" President Kanye screams into the mic.

"Ok Marshall, you only get one shot, don't miss this chance," he mutter under his breath as he pulls out the gun.

"And I wonder if you know."

Marshall's hand trembles.

"What it means?"

Emotion oozes from the speakers.

Tears form in Marshall's eyes.

"And I wonder... if you know..."

The crowd starts to erupt for the President as they all wave their hands.

Marshall puts the gun back in his pocket, and drops to his knees.

"What it means to find your dreams..."

Marshall pulls the trigger.

***

Marshall wakes up on his cot to the sound of bars slamming across from him. Groggily he gets up and uses the toilet that is in the corner of his cell. For the first time in years, a smile appears on the face, even if it is a slight one.

"You're getting some company today," a cop says while

opening up the cell door, leading another prisoner to share the tiny space with Marshall. "I'll let you two fight it out for the top bunk."

Marshall quickly finishes up using the toilet and turns around to introduce himself.

"Hey, I'm..God damn! Andre? How long has it been? I damn near forgot about you." Marshall goes to hug the man being put in the cell with him.

"Shit, I don't even know, what 12-13 years? Didn't think I'd ever see you again, let alone be paired up with you in here," Andre says reciprocating the hug.

"Well, don't get to used to me. They are only keeping me in here until they figure out what to do with me."

"And what do you expect them to do with you?"

"Shit, I'm an American hero now. Considering the former Prez was so egotistical that he refused to have a Vice President run with him, whoever get's put in charge will hopefully pardon me some point down the line. So I figure I'll do some time, be treated like a hero in here, and then go out and write a book about my life or some shit."

the shortest story in the history of ever

Emily Alberti

I just made eye contact with Liam for about one exact minute without blinking as he peaked at me over the back of a chair. I won the staring contest because then he tilted his head back and bent his body in as if being possessed by a poltergeist. His tail went straight and he leaped into the air out of the chair and darted himself at me. I maintained eye contact and this confused him even more so he ran to the other side of the apartment and then back to me in a swift action.

A Virgin in Paris
Joselyn Mejia

She watches the hand move second to second to
second until both hands reached twelve, releasing the
highly anticipated ring. She is the first to stand up, her
books already inside her Jansport. Before Ms. Wilson
can get a word in, she is out of the doorway only able
to hear a fragment of her insincere goodbyes. She can't
help but power walk across the halls, passing all the
familiar faces that she will be leaving behind on her trip
to Paris this summer. Bumping into her fellow
schoolmates, she manages to get a glimpse of Derek.
Once she spots him, she is lost in the abyss that is a
teenage girl's mind. Oh sweet beautiful Derek, her 24/7
much-welcomed distraction. She has had many Ben &
Jerry's, used Puffs tissues, and scratched "The
Notebook" nights pining over all the glances and smiles
she's had with her one true love. Like any teenage love
story, they've never spoken a word but that hasn't
stopped her from designing *Operation: Make Derek
Fall for Me* her mission once in Paris. She stands still,
paralyzed, once he begins to get closer. Before she
knows it, she's on the soda stained floor with an ache
on her back. Embarrassed she picks herself up and runs
straight home, not looking back to make sure Derek
hadn't seen. Once home, she only has and hour to
pack, going through every hanger, making sure she only
gets her best clothes to impress him. Showered and

131

ready to go, she alerts her mother that it's time. Once at the airport she makes her way across the crowd of tourists and gathers with the rest of the senior class. The instructor gives everyone their tickets and they all begin to find their seats. She finds her seat quickly, sits down and looks out the window. It's going to be and 11hr flight from Los Angeles to Paris. Since it's going to be a long flight, she begins to analyze every scenario possible that can lead Derek to fall for her. She spends most of the flight dreaming until they finally arrive at the airport. They don't take long to gather their belongings and head straight to their hotel. On the ride, she see all the marvelous buildings and shops that she would Google back home. The scenery makes her more anxious to begin her Derek plan. Once at the Hotel, the instructor gives the student's time to rest. The next day, they all gather at the lobby where they meet their travel guide. The guide begins to ask every student to introduce themselves with their names and zodiac sign for some reason. When it's her turn she introduces herself as Taylor and her sign as a Virgo. The guide then blurts out in his French accent "Virgin!" She is so embarrassed and like clockwork begins to turn red. The whole class begins to laugh and all she could do is smile and act like it's no bother. She turns around and see's Derek, holding hands with another girl. They both approach Taylor and for the first time he speaks to her saying, "Don't worry, you're in Paris, you're bound to get laid." With her softest voice she's can let out she says, "Yeah that was the plan." He smiles and walks away with the girl clinging to his waist leaving Taylor behind.

Girl

Joselyn Mejia

Lovely like a daisy
Sweet like honey
The light beyond the tunnel.

A child of innocence taken
Flowery face destroyed
Soul of kindness violated.

Five springs young
Eyes of hope now gone
Laid and exposed.

Skin pale like the moon
Lips a horrid purple
Hair still beautiful tornados.

A child too good
A child too pure
An angel.

White Walls
Megan Geis

White walls. That was the first thing the girl
noticed as she passed slowly through the open door.
The acrid stench of antibiotics burned her nose and
caused her eyes to tear. Still, even without the smell
tears would have come. She swept a hand over her
cheeks and swallowed her sobs as she stared,
heartbroken, at the scene in front of her.

"Dear?"
The girl's breath caught in her throat as her eyes
zeroed in on the red-headed woman in scrubs standing
before her. Instinctively, she backed away, bringing her
closer to the open door.
"Are you family?" The woman asked gently.
The girl nodded, her eyes wide.
A smile broke out on the woman's face. "You can come
closer, dear; you won't hurt him. We made sure he's as
comfortable as possible." She finished scribbling
something on her clipboard before placing it in the
holder at the end of the patient's bed. "I'll leave the
two of you alone, but not to worry! I'll only be a room
away if you need anything." She patted the girl on the
shoulder and ushered her closer to the chair right next
to the patient's bed, not noticing that her touch caused
the girl to flinch. Leaving the overwhelming smell of
perfume in her wake, the red-headed nurse left the
room.
The girl shifted tentatively as she tried to make herself
comfortable in the uncomfortable chair, but her eyes
kept lingering back to the machine on the other side of
the bed. It beeped rhythmically as a jagged line crawled

lazily across the black screen. She turned her attention then to the man in the bed. Slowly, she eased her hand closer to his; its angry, red scarring contrasted greatly with her pale, smooth skin. She traced her finger lightly over each puckered scar, each startling splash of bruising that plagued his right arm and hand. She gazed up at his face and bit her lip, fighting to control the waterworks. His left cheek was an ugly bluish-yellow color, and the wrinkled skin around his eyes sagged. His cheeks looked sunk in, the skin settling in uncomfortable waves along his face. The girl's eyes trailed down to his neck where blue and black bruises stuck out against the white pillow settled beneath his head of gray hair. It used to be brown and vibrant, the color of maple syrup as it dripped down from a tree. She couldn't believe it was him. He looked nothing like himself: a man full of life and adventure. Huddled underneath the thin sheets he looked weak. Vulnerable. She couldn't peel her eyes away from his injuries. His chest rose and fell slowly, his breathing the only sound besides the beeping of the machine.

"Daddy," the girl choked out. "Oh Daddy, I'm so sorry. I... I should have stopped you. I shouldn't have let you go!" She wrapped her hand around his. His was calloused but warm, the hand of a hardworking man and loving father. She brought the hand to her lips and kissed it, brushing it against her tearstained cheeks. Over the beeping of the machine, footsteps resonated from the hallway in through the open door. When she had entered the room, the hallways had been virtually empty. It was late, much too late for regular visitors, but she knew she wasn't imagining it. *He* was coming. Her back straightened as she sat up in the chair. The hairs on the back of her neck stood on end. She inhaled a trembling breath and released, trying to calm her frazzled nerves. She would not give him the satisfaction of seeing her scared. With a voice hard as steel, she spoke, "I thought you were going to wait outside. You said we didn't want to draw any attention. You're drawing attention." She was both surprised and delighted at the hint of annoyance she heard in her voice; it masked her fear nicely.

"I thought I could offer some assistance." The heavy footfalls on the linoleum floor echoed in the tiny space as he walked through the door.

"Haven't you done enough?" She spat out the words.

"Perhaps some motivation, then?" His deep voice rumbled, and she could feel the vibrations deep in her chest. Out of the corner of her eye, she tracked his movements as he moved to stand behind her. He was standing over her left shoulder, his hand hovering inches above the IV inserted in her father's arm. She lurched forward in her seat and grabbed his wrist before he had a chance to pull it out.

"You can't," she breathed, her heart pounding as her fingers dug into her antagonist's arm. "You need him alive."

"For now," the man replied, grabbing her hand and forcefully twisting it backwards.

She gritted her teeth. "He has to wake up on his own; I can't make him."

"Pity." He added more pressure to her arm.

She cried out, filled with self-loathing at giving him exactly what he wanted: her, in pain.

Suddenly, she felt a featherlike touch on her opposite wrist. The girl whipped her head around and watched as her father's fingers slowly developed a stronger grip around her forearm.

"Corinna?" Her father's voice was barely above a whisper that Corinna couldn't tell if she had imagined it or not.

"Daddy?" She whispered back. The hold on her throbbing wrist was released, and she turned fully to face the man lying in the bed. Corinna brought her aching arm around to rest her hand on top of her father's, sandwiching his warm hand between her cold palm and her arm.

The old man tilted his head in her direction, his eyelids twitching.

"Corinna?" He asked again, his voice hoarse but stronger this time.

"Yes!" Corinna cried. "Yes, Daddy, I'm here. I'm right here. Everything's going to be okay now."

"Baby, I can't see you. Why can't I see you?" His voice, panicked, scattered Corinna's insides.

"You're okay," she reassured him. "The doctor said that this is normal. You'll be able to see soon, I promise."

A slight breeze brushed against the back of her neck. *Oh, no.* She'd forgotten about *him*. The cool barrel of a gun smashed against her temple, causing her vision to swarm with little black dots. Corinna froze as her assailant leaned closer; his hot breath producing goosebumps on her skin.

"Remember why we're here, Corinna," he said.

"Corinna? What's wrong?" Her father asked, worry in his voice. The old man squeezed her arm, knowing something wasn't right. "Baby, what's going on?"

Corinna could hardly breathe. The gun cut deeper into her skin.

"Daddy, I'm fine-" her voice cracked. Her vision became blurry as even more pressure was applied. Oh god. She couldn't breathe.

"Corinna? Honey, what's happening?" Her father's voice was frantic now.

"I-" The cocking of the gun silenced Corinna, and she felt her father stiffen beside her.

"Who's there? What do you want?" The fragile voice was gone, and in its place was the intense, deep voice of her father, pre-hospital.

"Professor, we haven't met." The guy behind Corinna said as he held the gun steady against her temple. "But you have something I want, and I suggest you tell me where it is. Unless, of course, you want your daughter's brains splattered against these... *pristine* walls."

"What do you want?" Corinna's father asked again. Corinna felt the satisfaction practically oozing off her foe in waves. "Dad, don't-"

The gun bit more into her soft skin. She hissed her protest.

"Corinna, stop," her father commanded before turning his attention back to his invisible adversary. "What do you want from me?" He asked a third time.

"I want the map," the man said. "You give me the map, and I won't kill your daughter. You don't, well, you have a PhD. I think you could figure it out."

"You'll kill Corinna," her father replied, flatly. Corinna could feel more than see the cruel smile forming on her antagonist's face. "These walls are so dull," he said in reply. "They could use a little color, don't you think?"

10 Steps To Loving You. (Loving Someone With Mental Illness)
Jac Weitzel

Step One: Always let her pick the music in the car.
No matter how much you hate the Yeezus album,
Let her rap like Kanye, so you can love her like Kim.
The destination is more important than where you begin.

Step Two: Never make her choose.
Have the date planned
and arrive 30 minutes early,
because 30 minutes early is on time.
Which means I knew 30 minutes before
our first date that I would love you.

Step Three: Learn to read the users manual.
When she says "I come with a users manual."
Tell her you love her more.
Besides, designing the cover is what I'm
going to school for.

Step Four: Remind her why you love her.
I just do is not a good enough answer.
I love her because she taught me
to love myself.
She gave me a mirror
and taught me to love my reflection.
That was the hardest lesson.

Step Five: Don't ask.

She will laugh the whole way through,
she doesn't know why and neither will you.

But always ask for consent because
that's where things always went wrong.
So when you go to give her head
and she says no, cook her dinner instead.

Step Six: Always let her direct the correct
way to organize the book shelf.
For When her OCD says clean
instead of cuddle and watch TV.
Tell her the book shelf looks nice
organized by hight.
And always always let her direct
the correct way to organize the bookshelf.

Step Seven: Always be the one to order the pizza.
From talking on the phone to
asking the employee at the dollar tree
where the spoons are.
This is her anxiety.
Love her anyways,
and always be the one to order the pizza.

Step Eight: Hold her close.
On the days she can't get out of bed,
and the days she can't take one more step.
Hold her close.
Don't tell her everything will be okay
because she knows.

So on the days she just needs
10 more hours of sleep,
hold her close.

Step Nine: Move slowly.
Because when you go to grab her
face for a kiss she will flinch.
Understand that there were hands
that came before you
that weren't so peaceful.
That her rib cage hasn't
always been in one piece.
So when you go to grab her waste
to pull her in close,
remember to move slow.

Step Ten: Love her.
Just love her.

141

Bullets

Jac Weitzel

She hardly speaks,
but when she does.
Her words are bullets.
And instead
of being filled with tiny
pellets of metal.
They are filled with seeds.
Cause she is growing on me.

Grow me into a vine.
That stretches across
the whole garden.
So when you try to take me out,
I've touched every part of your life.
You can't get rid of me.
I'll be a pain in your ass.
Attached by my heart strings.

You'll have a huge box of my things,
buried in your closet.
With all of your skeletons,
and your dresses, your jeans,
and shoes.
And when you blow the dust off of me,
remember my guitar strings.

The way I used the stems of flowers
as tally marks,
for all the days I hadn't blown it yet.
So when I do.

Shoot your bullets in my dirt.
So your seeds can grow.
Don't worry about my garden,
being over grown by weeds.
Cause I quit sewing those seeds,
years ago.

I do not rely on your happy,
to make me happy.
I know I am weak,
at the knees.
Because everybody trips
over their own feet, sometimes.
How many people can say,
they've seen something
more beautiful than a sunset?

April Showers
didn't bring the flowers, darling.
Your heart did.

People You May Know

Jac Weitzel

I shouldn't be ashamed to be a woman.
Just like I shouldn't be ashamed to say
I was raped by one.
The focus is always on men.
But what about women who look like men.
How can you say I was asking for it
when I look like them?

You were 16, you should have known better.
Believe me, you don't have to give me
any more excuses about why it happened
than I already have.

I wish the cops would have done something.
I wish the *judge* would have know better.
I wish they both would have been there
the first time we smoked meth together.

Evidence?
I wonder if they would have needed more.
I wonder if they knew I never
watched porn before,
She showed me.

What about the empty bottle of
tequila on her night stand?
What if you can't stand?
Is that consent?

I wish I would have known what consent was.

I wish I would have told someone.
I wish she didn't tell me she loved me.
I wish I didn't believe that if I kept my mouth shut,
She would still love me.
I wish her name didn't show up in the
"people you may know"
section on Facebook.

But all this wishing,
doesn't make me feel better.
Turning you in,
wouldn't give justice
to all my suicide letters.

She told my friend
"I hope she's okay."
No. You don't get to
hope for anything
but the fucking rain.

I wonder if she thinks about it.
I wonder if she knows
the hole it left in my soul.
Or how many nights I
tore myself apart from
the skin.

Does she know how dirty
it makes me feel to let

anyone in.

God bless you.
Because hell is too good of
a place for people like you.
So instead of cutting myself,
I'm gonna cut this shit loose.
Now you can carry the weight,
of 4 years of hate built
into my bones.

I am sick and tired of
being sick and tired.
So this is my recovery poem.
Take it with you,
where ever you go.

Underneath an Oak Tree a Wooden Owl is Buried

Tim Bushika

Henry hadn't spoken a word since he entered his former childhood home. The silence that pervaded the house was thick. Every breath and movement was amplified, echoing through the bare interior. The stairs leading to the second floor creaked and cracked under his weight, threatening to give out. He moved more confidently once he reached the floor, following the narrow hallway to the attic stairs, the light from his flashlight closing the distance. Waves of cold air met him gradually as he ascended to the top floor.

His memory of the old attic was fairly precise, sans the dusty floors and windows. Cobwebs decorated the rafters, some of them even housing residents that comfortably spun their nets. October afternoon sunlight crept through the grimy and cracked north window. The orange light painted the rotting floorboards, and dust particles danced fluidly in the wash of luminescence. Henry drew in the minute details. He let his mind swell with images and words, wondering if he could compose a story about this particular afternoon.

It was inevitable, Henry concluded, that he would someday return to this particular house, now uninhabited and forgotten; the same house with ivy vines bordering the west wall, shingles that melted lazily from the roof, and the brown and leafless bushes that guarded the anterior of house, their branches like

147

the jagged teeth of a predator. The house hadn't always been intimidating and decrepit; there had been a time when people *wanted* to live there, to inhabit its walls and to fill its confines with their voices.

The day before, Henry had taken a long drive around his college town when he decided to leave its borders and let the highway take him as far as possible from the comfort of his surroundings. Depression had been seeping in since he learned of his mother's cancer diagnosis, and because of the mental strain he grew quieter than ever. The road had become his best friend, and on the weekends he would drive all over the state searching for something he couldn't place. This particular weekend he followed a route that seemed vaguely familiar and came upon his old neighborhood in which he stumbled upon the house, settled near the end of the road. It seemed to exert a magnetic force that pulled Henry towards it, and he didn't resist. Since the house was deserted he decided that it wouldn't hurt to poke around, and see what he could find.

And digging through stacks of moth-chewed cardboard, Henry found nostalgia. Piled in a dusty box were the books his parents used to read on the back porch during long summer afternoons. Most of them were science fiction novels about alien civilizations and ghostly encounters. Henry beamed; it became clear where the seeds of his interest in the paranormal had been planted.

Next to him was a shoebox full of loose papers. Most of them were bound with paper clips and staples. Written on them in pencil and ink were Henry's original stories. Some were totally illegible, only to be decoded by a six-year-old mind. Others were written in plain English, and were moderately decent drafts. Henry hungrily ruffled through these narratives, mildly disappointed to discover that these pieces held more imaginative qualities than most of his adult stories.

Gingerly depositing the papers Henry caught a glimpse of a chest filled with toys. Among them were Power Ranger action figures, metal Slinky rings, and his handheld video game collection. He picked up one of the handhelds and pressed the power switch, holding his breath. The indicator light flashed green and the screen brightened. Henry's mouth dropped open and he let out a sharp laugh. Killing the power, he placed the handheld back in the box.

As he was about to pull away his hand brushed past an object. It was an item that he had not seen in years. Henry furrowed his brow, his gaze fixed on the mysterious carving. It was a wooden owl, intricately carved with sharp details. The animal was perched on a flat base, silky soft on the bottom. The weight was about what Henry expected, maybe a bit heavier. He felt that the owl had belonged to someone he knew, but he couldn't place whom. Could it have been from a friend at school? Henry's grandfather was a carpenter but he was doubtful that his grandfather could carve a piece this intricate. He tilted his head and ran his fingers over the curves and lines of the owl's body.

Tucking the owl into his coat pocket he continued to rummage through boxes, finding one labeled "PARENTS." Buried under various layers of musty clothing he unearthed a photo album. Henry sifted through it. The photos were nothing special. Henry recalled taking a few with various disposable cameras. Strange angles and poor lighting threatened each of his compositions. He ventured deeper into the glossy memories.

But eventually his stomach dropped. He had come across a photo his mother had taken. Henry was posing at the tree line of the house's backyard, toy dump trucks and action figures littered at his feet. Adjacent to him was a white mist that barely resembled a small child. A tiny hand protruded from the anomaly.

Henry gasped.

At first he thought it was a trick of the camera but the lighting was too dim. The mist was well defined, with some blue shades covering the mid to lower half of the figure. A chill ran down his spine as Henry suddenly realized what, or rather whom, it was. It had been a young girl, around the age of twelve (at least when Henry knew her, though he remembered how she never aged). She had apparently posed with him for a photograph in the backyard. His parents knew her as Henry's imaginary friend, which didn't seem all that unusual given that he was an only child. But here she was on film, an apparition.

And her name was Abigail.

Thirteen years had lapsed since Henry had last seen, spoken to, or even thought about Abigail. Despite the time gap vivid memories of their friendship came rushing forward. The first day they met, when she emerged from the hallway and sat on Henry's bedroom floor opposite him, barely making a sound. The numerous days they spent exploring the hidden corners of the house; Abigail had shown him nooks and crannies no adult could ever see the way they could. Their hikes to the giant oak tree just beyond the backyard; walking there and back, Henry recalled, used to take up most of the afternoon. Abigail had seemed fond of the tree as she often dubbed it as her "anchor" to the world, a metaphor that still mystified Henry.

Denial ran through him, but he couldn't hide the truth. She was a ghost. The hairs on the back of Henry's neck stood on end. As if on cue footsteps moved along the hardwood of the second floor hallway toward the attic. Henry gripped the sides of the photo album, ears perked.

Instinctually he called, "Hello? Is anybody there?"

The footsteps stopped abruptly. It seemed impossible, but the sound of his own voice had frightened Henry more than the footsteps themselves. His words violently cut the established silence. Until then he hadn't registered how quiet it was inside the house. It's an old house, he thought to himself. Must have misinterpreted the foundation settling.

Drinking in a deep breath Henry slid the photo from its plastic and folded it, slipping it into the same pocket as the owl. He emptied a small box of his father's baseball cards into the old toy bin and set the photo album inside the box that previously held the cards. Gently he placed his father's record player on the album along with a few vinyl records (*Abbey Road, Dark Side of the Moon*, the greatest hits of Queen's catalog, some Miles Davis classics, *The Breakfast Club* soundtrack, and a couple of old radio shows), the handheld video game, a few game cartridges, and a crimson red summer dress his mother used to wear.

Lifting the box of treasures Henry gingerly descended the attic stairs, mindful of his footing. He moved down the hallway towards the stairs that led to the first floor, sneaking a glance into his old bedroom. He did a double take, thinking that he had seen Abigail staring up at him from the carpet, the early morning sunlight reflecting off her pale skin and igniting her golden curls, a shy smile playing at the corners of her lips. But neither she, nor her apparition, were present.

As he marched downstairs Henry silently lamented the bare wall along the staircase. Once there had been photos of him and his parents, extended family, and friends placed in tasteful frames on the wall. Now it was bare, devoid of color or life. Reaching the bottom he hastily snuck glances into the living room and kitchen areas, knowing that, like the wall, there wasn't much to see.

He shuffled outside and lifted open the trunk of his Subaru, depositing the box. Shutting it, he patted his coat using both hands, trying to locate the car keys when he felt the owl's wooden body. Grasping the wooden sculpture he glanced at the sky. Dusk was approaching and dark clouds were rolling in.

Once again Henry considered Abigail's puzzling "anchor" metaphor about the oak tree. He unlocked the driver's side door as a warm wind brushed past his pant leg. Looking up he noticed a dark figure just beyond the tree line in the backyard. They made eye contact but the figure dashed, leaves crunching under its stride. Without much hesitation Henry ran toward the woods, not sure why he felt compelled to chase after the shadow.

*

He chased the shadow to the oak tree where it, along with the noise it made, disappeared. When it came to the oak tree's size, Henry's memories had not betrayed him. He might have thought it was big when he was a child, but now he could see that the tree was immense. The width of its trunk alone was easily ten feet in diameter; its summit extended far beyond the other trees. He had to strain his neck for a glimpse of the top. The backs of the oak's leaves were exposed to the wind, a sure sign of rain.

Kneeling at the base of the tree, Henry laid his hand on the trunk.

He reached into his coat pocket and fetched the wooden owl. Laying it gently on a large root, Henry swept away the dead leaves in front of the oak and inspected for dirt. He yanked his hand back suddenly. Something had cut him; blood seeped from an open wound on the web between his index finger and thumb. Using his other hand he unearthed a weathered and rugged concrete slab hidden under the mess of bramble and leaves. He read the inscription while licking his wound: *Abigail James Nordstrom. Born 1924. Died 1937. Taken too soon, but forever in our hearts.* Henry lowered his wounded hand, setting it on the cold stone; a bloody dot formed next to "1937."

He sighed, closing his eyes and letting the cold

153

autumn air move through him.

Digging a hole next to Abigail's grave, Henry lowered the owl inside and slowly covered the carving with dirt and broken leaves.

The wind suddenly picked up and chilled his bones. He could hear a faint exhale close by. After a silent prayer, Henry garnished the owl's grave with a tiny crucifix formed with twigs. Pulling his coat around him he left the tree, stumbling through the brush and struggled to find the footpath.

As he reached the border of the backyard and the woods he stopped and sat on the invisible median. He felt that none of the houses he lived in held the same sort of mystery, excitement, or curiosity as this one. And perhaps, he considered, it was for the sole reason that his family never owned it to begin with. Abigail was its rightful heir and, Henry figured, she had allowed them to stay there in exchange for his friendship.

In some way Henry didn't want her to be at peace, not yet. He desperately wanted to talk with her again, now comfortable with the idea of their strange friendship. He waited for the shadow to appear behind him, or for activity to occur within the house, such as the toss of a curtain, or a peculiar noise.

Dark clouds soon suffocated the evening sky. Rain fell swiftly and in unapologetic amounts. The trees and grass sucked in the moisture gratefully. The wood of the old house moaned and creaked as the water cleansed its rough exterior. Birds sought shelter under thick canopies of leaves in treetops, shaking off the moisture from their wings.

Henry was soaked, but he didn't mind. There was time. He could wait.

10 Steps to Loving Me [A Severe Introvert]

Lauren Elizabeth

Step 1: patience is key
we will be in busy places and social situations
and i will need you more than ever.
my fears are irrational but please whisper "youre okay"
and make sure your hand never leaves my waist
because your touch is comfortable.
Patience is key.

Step 2: Don't compliment me
even though i love it when you say i'm beautiful
and you love the smell of my hair
i will always laugh
and brush it off with a quiet thanks.
i love it when you say these things.
i probably need it more but just for my sake
don't compliment me anymore.

Step 3: know that i'm going to annoy you.
i'm the only person who will notice
the way you drink your coffee
or that eyelash on your cheek
i will pick out things you want to forget
but that's just because i love the things you don't.
i will cherish all these things and hope you do the same
know that i'm going to annoy you.

Step 4: ill need to borrow your strength
there will be days when i cant get out of bed
and you'll roll over to kiss me

but instead you'll need to wipe my tears
and let the sun in
ill hate you at first but it's exactly what i need
ill need to borrow some of your strength

Step 5: just leave me alone
and when i say this i mean it
ill need many moments to myself
even if i was clingy last week
i promise its not you
just leave me alone please

Step 6: touch me
i may hate social situations
but that does not mean i dont crave the human touch.
dont kiss me in public
but if we're at home you better be holding me
i need you to touch me

step 7: dont as me what i'm thinking
ill giggle in the middle of you going down on me
thats a given
but dont stop to ask why
because i dont know 98% of the time
and the other 2% of the time im too in love with you to
even communicate so
just dont ask me what im thinking

step 8: dont make me choose
and dont even ask me to
even if it's only for the soundtrack or bar for date night
it may seem like a small request
but to me it's almost the end of the world
so make sure you have the plans set

dont make me choose.

step 9: remind me why
remind me why you chose me
because i could pick 100 others
100 others who dont come with a users manual
100 others who will love going out with your friends
and make decisions
so please
remind me why

and step 10: dont stop loving me
even though its inevitable
and just thinking about it tears me to pieces
but i get attached too easily and fall too hard
 i will worry about this every night
because the honest truth is
i love you more than you will ever know
and cant picture a day without you in my life.
even after all of this
please dont stop loving me.

Left Out (In the Cold)
Lauren Elizabeth

My tears hit the floor
harder than the rain that pounded
on the pavement outside.

My hands trembled more
than the trees in
the storm's wind.

And I felt lost
in it all.
As the thunder and lightning
took over the night's sky,
the darkness and depression
did the same to my mind.

I was lost and alone with
no coat or umbrella
slowly getting sicker and sicker
while you were safe and sound
in the warmth of your room.

And oh how I wished
you could be a coat wrapped around me
or the umbrella giving me shelter
from it all.

But you were what caused
this storm to rage on
you were the reason for
the dark cloud over my head.

And with all that I had
I wished I could go inside.

But I chose to stay out
and catch a cold
because I loved the sound of the thunder
and the rain on my skin
but it made me so sick
I could barely crawl to safety.

Walk Beside Me
Lauren Elizabeth

The monsters under my bed
don't scare me
as much as the ones inside my head.
The monsters inside
will kill us all
if we allow them to.

You can use whatever you want to shoo them away,
a line of mystery,
a pill with power,
a cut to let them loose,
or everything all at once

all at once, all at once
it may kill you all at once
but that's what we want, right?

That's what I thought
at 2am
alone in a city flat
high on whatever the medicine cabinet held.
It's 2am and the monster inside my head
is sitting right beside me
with no intention of walking
out the door.

It's 2:30 now
and I've finally found the flashing exit sign
to push him out.
Or so I thought.

A day later,
room of all white,
the monster looking from the foot of the bed.
Defeated and angry
I ask why
why, why, why

we try to kill the monsters in our head
but we end up killing ourselves instead.

We want to kill us when we need to walk hand in hand
in simultaneous harmony
because we can exist
we can, we can, we can
with the monster sitting right beside us.

In Your Arms
Nick Bucci

Benjamin Walsh heard the call to attention and straightened his back, rifle coming to stand by his heel. Beside his bunkmate, Kelley Smith, Benjamin stood in line of battle in the 28th Massachusetts, alongside the rest of the "Irish" Brigade, under General Thomas Meagher. His regiment carried the only green flag into battle; Benjamin looked to it for inspiration. The other regiments had had their colors sent north and requested refurbished colors.

Ahead, in the distance, the grey Confederate line nestled itself along the equally grey stone wall in a sunken road. Firing at the approaching Union lines, they made quick work of the foolish men marching up the hill. There was little the Yankees could aim at, except for the occasional exposed head and forage cap. Brigade by brigade, and regiment by regiment, the Union lines crumbled until the call came down to fend for yourself. Soldiers cursed the name Burnside and prayed for the return of McClellan, who would led them to victory. Through the rain of lead and shell fragments, Union boys headed back to cross the stream into Fredericksburg. Many would lie beneath the stars tonight, among their dead comrades, too fearful to run and attract a bullet in the back.

"Irish Brigade! At the double-quick. Forward! *March!*" Meagher ordered.

Heading out of town, the brigade soon began to arrive on the field, heralding a renewed vigor of Confederate artillery. They found a brief respite in a shallow ravine by the muddy stream. There, Meagher had the Irishmen fix bayonets and prepare to charge. Benjamin Walsh withdrew the pointed metal weapon and affixed it to the end of his smoothbore barrel. *Clink! Clink! Clink!* echoed down the line. Benjamin knew that fixing bayonets assures close combat and does something to the body of those preparing. Even in training, the bayonet drills quickened his heart, alerted his senses, and blood ran cool through his veins.

Benjamin and Kelley look up into the skies and pray. Benjamin closes his eyes and sees the faces of his wife and newborn child, at home in Boston. Cradling young Maggie in her arms, his wife, Jill, smiles at him. Benjamin leans down and kisses Jill on the forehead. The baby girl yawns and cuddles closer to her mother, melting into the warmth of the blanket. The proud parents smile widely at each other. Interrupted by Meagher, Benjamin returned to reality and looked ahead, ready for the fight.

"If I should die," Meagher shouted above the din of shells flying overhead, "I shall know that I died fighting for the right cause. Today, we fight for the American Republic; tomorrow we fight for Ireland." *Aye, General! I'll see you in Galloway!* Benjamin whispered.

After three cheers, the brigade moved forward into the line of fire. A thicket of lead impacted with the Union line, felling dozens at one time. The need to crawl or turnabout ran through the head of Benjamin, but not a man returned to safety; instead, they marched further into the grim face of death. Beside Benjamin, Kelley groaned and fell like a rag doll, both his legs shattered. Fifty yards from the grey line, Benjamin finally took the chance to fire back. However, it was bittersweet upon seeing the flags of fellow

Irishmen.

"You're on the wrong side!" Benjamin shouted.

Just two minutes passed, but dozens were dead and hundreds wounded, streaming back to the town. Finally, sick of the unnecessary carnage, Meagher made the order: "Retreat!" Retiring to the rear, Benjamin fired one last round and turned to run. He fled past the writhing body of Kelley, his face contorted in pain, eyes open. Before the ravine, he felt a train drive through his back, and twist through his chest. Benjamin's eyes shot open and he faltered in his sprint, throwing his musket up. Collapsing on the cold grass and dirt, he saw the weapon land amid the bodies of his comrades, friends.

The cold seeped into him, beginning where the slug had entered his back. As the blood left his body, the cold replaced it, swarming in like a hive of bees. Lying next to him, Jill smiled. She stroked his cheek and whispered soft words. Benjamin couldn't hear and he wheezed for her to speak up. Taking his hand and drawing it down to her stomach, she said something intelligible. Benjamin looked up into her face and nodded in understanding.

"I'm pregnant."

A tear ran down Benjamin's scruff, clearing a trail through the black powder. Jill became much warmer as he turned to ice, an unlivable environment. The sky turned dark, while Jill lit candles around them. She came back down by him and whispered again.

"Let's have another one."

Grinning, she kissed him softly and took Benjamin to sleep. Jill's moans drowned out those of the wounded as they lay in the December night, freezing to death. In the warm bed, surrounded by candles,

Benjamin was protected from the crying and the occasional gunshot that ended a groan. The mist shrouded the dead and dying along the field, while Benjamin and Jill were enshrined by the bright unshielded light of candles. Jill spoke first, as they lay together.

"You have to wake up so you can come back to me."

Benjamin opened his eyes and looked confused at her.

"I am with you, Jill."

"You're not truly with me, Benjamin. Wake up and come back to me."

Benjamin nestled closer into her, kissing Jill's neck.

"I love you," Benjamin said.

"I'll see you soon, Benjamin."

Shaking him, Jill looked into his eyes.

"Wake up, Benjamin."

The candlelight became dull and, opening his eyes, Benjamin saw dark clouds overhead. He was surrounded in a blanket, coated in blood. When he tried to move his head, a sharp pain ran up his back. He yelled, which only brought on more pain. The two men on either side, carrying the body, were shocked to find this one alive. How had he survived the night? Looking in the blue wool blanket, they saw a Yankee in agonizing pain, his mouth open, eyes strained shut. Benjamin's brown hair was matted down with dirt and his blouse was stained with the blood of his friends and his own body. The men holding him had already taken his shoes, a precious treasure on the Confederate side.

"Hey Yank! We didn't think you'd be alive," the man in front said.

"Yeah! Billy here is right. You looked mighty

dead," Reb number two added.

"I feel dead," Benjamin croaked.

"Well, once we get you to the hospital in town, I'm sure you'll get to go home," Billy said.

"I sure hope so. My wife and little girl are waiting for me."

The walk to the nearby field hospital was peaceful compared to the misery of the cramped waiting area. Outside of the brick building, a pile of freshly amputated limbs was oozing steam in the cold air. A small smile formed on Benjamin's face at the thought that they can't amputate a back; it was quickly stripped as the smell of wounds, gunpowder, and blood wafted into his nostrils. He held back the urge to vomit, but a bit of acid ran up his throat and touched his tongue.

Instructions for Your Apartment
Nick Bucci

Cracking an egg involves several stages of grief. Observe the shell. It is whole and smooth. *Denial*. As your hand clutches the coolness, it almost feels wet, slippery. In a fowl swoop, you slam the egg onto the edge of a frying pan. *Anger*. You see a shell has decided to stay with the nutrients that you intend to consume. Fetch it. *Bargaining.* You burn your finger trying to work the shell bit out of your food. *Depression.* You decide that just one little piece of shell shouldn't ruin your morning. *Acceptance.*

After this, the author will write some instructions on something silly like crying, winding a clock, or how to sing. In fact, the author will expedite this introduction so as to have a large amount of instructions on things you should already understand how to do. Proceed, idiot.

How to Brawl

This is the only way, it seems, that your friends are capable of hanging out. You have tried for movie nights, to watch one of the Austin Power's films. You end up, alone, dropping shots of rum into your gullet, jealous of Austin Power's mojo: his ability to interact with people. You try to start a new run through of *Fallout 3* and put your charm all the way up. Fantasize about being the perfect social animal.

The only way to win at *Super Smash Bros* is to play

as Kirby and to listen to the sound of mashing buttons and shouts filled with curses. In this way you will fuck up the other players. Even if they all play as their favorite character: Nate is Snake, Christopher is King Dedede, Luke is Zelda, and Tonner is Captain Falcon, Kirby will succeed. Even though you lack the tactics and have no idea what the fuck you are doing, Kirby will overcome. You will whack them with your big ass hammer and fuck them up. However, failing to pick Kirby still leaves open the option of handing the controller to someone else. If you can't handle the cute pink round ball of cuteness, get the fuck out! End lesson.

Chilling on the Roof

This is your first apartment. You found two other people, Chris and Matt, who have agreed to cohabitation with you. The landlord is difficult to understand, but you try to be kind since she is from a country in Southeast Asia; you forget which one. Matt has a room to himself, justifying a decrease in how much you and Chris should pay for internet. Chris and you occupy the other bedroom, which is quite large. Later on, your friend Nate will join the lease. Three is almost too much for the room, no matter the size. You went to high school with Chris and feel comfortable around him. After the first two months, you hear about a lunar eclipse. You excitedly tell Chris, showing the article on Facebook.

Living in a two-story apartment, you must open the window of your bedroom to the roof of your porch.

The first time is an attempt to see the rare lunar eclipse after reading and anticipating the occurrence. You bend under the window and step onto the tin metal, which is rusting in some places. Avoid those spots. The roof indents where you put your foot, loudly proclaiming your presence. A bird flutters off hastily. You look up, hoping to see the eclipse. No luck because of that damned cloud cover.

The second time you venture onto the roof will be with your roommate to hang out and talk. You smoke weed for the first time, after a long time considering his offer. You don't get high.

"Was I supposed to inhale?" You ask.

Your roommate laughs loudly, like he is about to hack out a hair ball. He nods. Nevertheless, the stars are beautiful with the broken street lights. When you go out again, try to bring out the Wii for Brawl. Refer back to **How to Brawl** on how to play.

How to Deal With Boredom

Really? Are you that lonely? Take a book and place it against the wall. You may have the binding touch the wall, the cover, the back; if you want to be a badass, open it to a random page and touch the wall. Take that page, find a sentence, and come up with a story. Your main character, Joe, will be the most charming guy with any woman of his choice. His friends even *offer* to watch Austin Powers. Shit! This is non-fiction.

Easter By Yourself

When your parents and brother have left on *their* break to the family timeshare Virginia (which happens to not correspond with your college break) indulge in homework. The sensation of Creative Nonfiction, an English paper, Marine Biology Presentation, and French translations is immense. You are alone. With only Frank Sinatra and Dean Martin to keep you company and time flying, do your best to complete all your assignments in one day.

Friday, you had to work security, making sure nobody stole computers or board games at GameFest. You realize that no one is foolish enough to try and take something with dozens of college kids around. This is a chance for nerds to hang out for twelve hours straight. Thankfully, you are only required to keep an eye out until one in the morning and there's free pizza. Instead of going to sleep, you find Nate, Tonner, and Luke playing *Munckins: The Good, The Bad, The Munchkin*. You join them until five and then drag yourself to bed. You don't wake up until two in the afternoon on Saturday, which turns into an unproductive day.

Now, it is Sunday and you feel swamped, unsure where to start. You jot down a to-do list, identifying which projects require immediate attention. They are all due either Monday or Tuesday. The likelihood of you completing the tasks at hand are slim. You feel fucked. Not just by the professors unintentionally assigning everything at once, but at yourself for not doing something Saturday. Good game!

Instructions on Concentration

Ignore the laughs and excitement coming from downstairs. It's just more *Smash Bros*. You hear footsteps. Nate crashes through the door (though not literally, he merely throws open the precipice to your room). He demands you to come downstairs. You tell him you'll be down. He leaves. Crank out the last page of your present assignment and run down. It may not be the *best* lab report, but bonding with friends is much healthier for you.

The Wedding
Olivia Cyr

An addition to Denis Johnson's short story, "Dirty Wedding"

Back when Michelle and I might have known what we were doing, we decided to get married.

We got married two, maybe three years before she got pregnant. It was a small one, the type that only had a few seats available for any family the bride and groom still had left. It was snowing, and Michelle had been worried that some awful thing would happen, that our car wouldn't start on the way to the Wellington Avenue United Church of Christ.

It was before the Holy water, before the mess that was our relationship when Michelle stopped loving me.

We'd been sitting in the kitchen, her eating from a bowl of soup, leaning her bony weight on one elbow, stirring wildly with the other hand, and listening to me read from the newspaper.

She stopped me when I got to one thing.

"Hold on," she set the spoon down. "Read that last part again."

"What?" I flipped the page, scouring the article.

"The lines you just read, just now," she urged me to read again, wagging her hand.

I turned the page, and flopped my legs back over one of the kitchen chairs. It was an article about a kid who'd been shot in the south side.

When I'd finished reading that the kid's name was Ali, and that he was fifteen, Michelle took to her tomato soup again. It was chunky, with little bits of old bread floating around in it that she'd torn up and sprinkled in. We were poor but we had a kitchen I liked to cook in, and she had to eat whatever I tried to make. I needed her to be happy, but it was hard.

Michelle sat back, looking into her bowl. "Well shit."

I slid the article toward her, sniffed, and stood up.

"Are you coming?" I'd already scooped up a cotton swab from the counter and was looking at her, her at the table with her head bent over the soup.

She stood and followed me into the bathroom, sat on the toilet seat and watched me go to work.

"Shit," she said softly. "Fifteen. Little baby boy."

***

Michelle looked like she had been sacked in the gut, already having vomited. I was trying to be just fine, making her look me in my eyes, telling her things to make her laugh and get her to listen to me.

In the mirror, I had rings under my eyes but was lucid

enough to splash water from the dingy sink onto my cheeks.

Afterward, we lay on the bed watching some messed up television show with the volume muted. Michelle had her arm draped over my chest, breathing sourly onto my cheek and ear, in and out of watching the television and falling asleep.

I wanted to chuck the remote at the window suddenly to wake her up. Or shout that the black family had won a thousand and eight-hundred dollars on the game show that had just ended. She was beginning to drool onto my sleeve, so I wrenched myself out from under her, placed her arm by her torso, and shut the door behind me.

On the train, the doors kept opening for these kids, all dressed in denim and hollering, sitting down fast on their seats and jabbering to one another. Street kids. Probably riding around to get away. They all had bobble heads and big huge eyes, like fast and huge animals. They were all sixteen and eighteen and some twenty-one, probably, doped up and scared but not showing it.

A girl about twelve was riding with them, and she seemed to be their silent leader, maybe a kid sister of one of the boys. She had these perfect white tennis shoes and smooth yellowy skin, warm caramel on the Night Diamond.

The train halted hard, and the girl slithered off the seat and looked at the others, and they followed, hooting and bustling through the doors and walking off into the station, then out into the dark city. I wondered how old she was, if she was supposed to be out so late. That girl's smooth curly ponytail bobbed as she walked behind them, and she turned, for a second, back to me on the train before it took off, then set herself wayward and went on.

***

It didn't take me very long to discover that Michelle knew the Ali kid who'd been gunned down, and she spent a whole day holding herself with one arm wrapped around her body, as if the whole thing of it would fall apart and drop off one limb at a time. We'd heard from the neighbor that he was involved in some messy deal and knew too much, and after he bought some stuff someone drove by and shot him, twice, in the back.

She'd falter when I asked what I should make for breakfast, then take the hot option, saying in a light voice, "toast."

Ali was one of Michelle's tutees when she worked for the city school system a couple days a week before we knew each other. She would ride the train to the city, and walk the two miles to the school's lower level where the inner-city kids had their afterschool program. I knew she read to them, showed them how to do math problems, but she'd never been good at her own times tables.

Ali was just a kid, I knew, one she'd spent the most time on, months, even. She would know the shriveling loss, the absence of something like a soul, before she would know she had it in her to grieve.

"It's a job," she'd said once, shrugging, when I asked her if she was sure she knew how to tutor a kid. "I'll survive. They'll survive."

She liked tutoring in the city, even before we were a couple. We weren't living in the same apartment yet but we'd been on a few coffee dates, and that was the first and last thing she ever told me about herself. I wasn't supposed to care about her and I didn't, not more than I had to. She'd started after seeing a flyer posted by the union station, and came home Tuesday and Friday nights at four-thirty on the dot. She'd toss herself on a chair in the kitchen without kissing me, and I'd make us something good to keep things nice, and fuzzy.

Her principle thanked her for the work she did by sending a greeting card in the mail with his loopy signature, which she opened, skimmed, and tossed on the junk pile. It was her first job and they fired her for showing up late, "unable to work with the students under appropriate and safe circumstances." I'd reached for the card with curiosity, half-wanting a reaction out of her that at least showed she was fed up, but she swiped it, and dropped it in the trash can. Later, we made love and I lit myself a cigarette I didn't smoke while she cried into my shirt and asked if there was any dope left.

***

It was that evening, at the table, when Michelle was

stirring her soup and I was looking at her blonde hair and back again at my newspaper, that I had a thought.

"What if we got married?"

Michelle kept stirring and looked at me. "What?"

"What if we did? Get married. Would you marry me?"

She thought about that for a long while, pushing the bowl from one index finger to the other, the bottom rim leaving water marks on the table's surface.

"Sure, sure," she said absently.

I'd looked at her for a moment after she said that, unsure why I had asked and more unsure why she'd agreed, and then wondered how much of the soup she was going to eat. Then I'd taken to the paper again and asked if I could read aloud for a bit.

***

The day of, I spent a full hour riding the trains, getting on, getting off, watching people's eyes watching buildings pass, watching billboards, watching me. All going somewhere and ending up just shy of nowhere, and then passing into darkness before the big swallowing of it all as the cars got sucked into tunnel after tunnel.

I wasn't nervous, but the wedding wasn't going to be a big deal. Sure, it was going to *mean* something, but

Michelle wasn't ready to love me how she was bound to, before I became who I was, and while I was still finding out who that *actually* was.

How do you know what will happen if the future keeps getting sucked into blackness before you can even see the fingers of it? How will you know if you'll like it, if you'll live?

***

At the church, Michelle and I stood in front of a man who looked like a reverend. He was balding and short, stocky with broad shoulders, and very thin from the waist down. He looked like a weeble-wobble, and spoke too slow. We were wed in the church lobby, because it was cheaper that way and there was a distilled water dispenser in the corner, and a stack of little cups on the table beside it. I'd picked our venue; told Michelle it would be nice to have it quiet and inexpensive, and she'd agreed by looking absently at her red sundress and brown sandals in the bedroom mirror. Michelle was absent when I told her the car would be fine on the ride to the church a few blocks over. She'd spent a while telling me with curse words that I should have gotten it fixed months ago, but when I moved her gently with my hand into the passenger seat, she stopped all conversation. She was absent on the drive over, she was absent during the default vows —she was absent in red and ready to run fast.

Michelle's two brothers, her Aunt Sarah, and her three

girl cousins sat in folding chairs, all fanning themselves with their crushed paper water cups. In the chairs on my side were my mother, my mother's half-sister, my half-Aunt Krista, and her five-year old daughter, Kerrie. During the ceremony they were quiet, respectful, and fidgeting. Everyone was sweating and unhopeful. We were ringed, and I kissed Michelle's cheek. We didn't talk about the wedding after it happened.

***

We didn't get married because it felt *right.* And we didn't because we were in love, or even because we wanted to.

I'd asked Michelle because I thought it would give her something to do, something to wake up every day and *be*. If she didn't love me, she could look like she did. I thought I'd like to see her like that.

Tired of her sitting in the kitchen, while we were living on the east side and without a clue, I gave her a clear, level-eyed out. I'd set up a question, then watched her face to see the whites of her eyes disappear, to hear the shrillness of her voice, or maybe see the shake of her head while she tossed me a look that said, *don't fuck around*, and yet there she was, nodding and stirring without seeing the opening.

She'd boarded the train with me, tied herself to me in her word, and said, "Sure." It was all into the rushing dark from there.

Jerold Harvey Took the Stairs
Alan Rose

It was a Wednesday, March 14th to be exact. A quick glance outside told him all he needed to know about the weather for the day. He saw how his fellow citizens of New York City had ditched their thick jackets in favor of more fashionable clothes, and noticed that the streets were a little bit fuller than they had been the week before. He knew this meant that the low winter temperatures were slowly warming to their spring averages.

Jerold liked the cold, however. He embraced it, enjoyed the way it felt to be wrapped up in big coats and jackets. He liked being able to sink into what he was wearing, to be enveloped by the fabric as if he were in an invisibility cloak. What he really liked most about the cold was how many people elected to take a cab or subway to their destinations instead of walk. On the most frigid of days, when the wind chill could make the "real" temperature flirt with numbers at or below zero, he often times found himself walking alone. Not that it mattered much. For Jerold, he was always alone.

He didn't have many friends. Only a select few people at his job knew his name, and he wasn't one hundred percent sure his boss was one of them. Jerold didn't mind though. It wasn't that he didn't like other people, or even that he didn't get along with others. If someone took to the arduous task of getting to him, they normally ended up liking him. The problem was Jerold's crippling fear of exposing himself to the world. Not in a predatory afternoon special on Dateline type of way, but in a personal way. He hated the thought of rejection, of putting a thought or idea out into the world and having it shut down and returned to him. He never told jokes, not out loud at least. Just the possibility of having a joke go un-laughed at was enough for him to refrain from even the most basic comedic quips. Jerold was trapped inside of himself.

It was 7:15 when he stepped outside. Work didn't start until 8:30, but Jerold always walked the 14 blocks instead of fetching a cab. He tried it once, riding in a cab. Everything was going fine until the driver had the audacity to ask him how his day was going. Jerold didn't have it in him to ask the gentleman to pull over, so he reluctantly engaged in chit-chat for the five minute ride. When he got to the office that day, he had sweated through his shirt.

Jerold cast his eyes downward as he waded through the throngs of businessman and visitors that crowded his daily route. He figured he could make the walk blindfolded if he had to. Sometimes after making accidental eye contact with a stranger, he considered it.

When he got to his office building, he was out of breath. In no way shape or form was Jerold in good shape. His legs turned to jelly not even halfway on his walk, and his back ached from where his spine veered off to the right just above the small of his back. He wore a film of sweat on his forearms and forehead. The building had forty-eight floors, with Jerold's company, NewTech, operating from floors 11 – 18. Most of his co-workers sold and marketing cutting edge televisions and tablets, while Jerold answered support chats for struggling customers. There were six elevators that serviced the building, carrying clients and employees to their desired destination within seconds. A ride up the elevator would mean a chance for Jerold to catch his breath, to rest from his long walk while being lifted to the floor where he would spend the next nine hours or so answering chat messages from customers that were too dimwitted to figure out how to set up their new television or connect to their cable box. However, a ride up the elevator would include being stuck with other people in a confined space. The awkward silence would rip him apart, being stuck so close to other people he was unfamiliar with could make him faint. Quite simply, an elevator was a living hell for Jerold.

So Jerold Harvey took the stairs. Every day when he came into the office lobby he would walk past the people waiting for an elevator and head straight to the stairwell. He was sure that people stared, that anyone from his company that knew of his routine found him odd. Why would the gimpy kid with the sweaty skin skip a leisurely ride up twelve floors and opt to walk them instead? For Jerold it was a no-brainer. No one in the building ever used the stairs, so for him it was another five minutes alone. He could count on one hand the number of times he had passed someone, though each incident made his heart stop.

As Jerold got closer to the twelfth floor, he prepared himself mentally for the day ahead. Wednesday's were never extremely busy for him. He would most likely spend most of the day reclining in his office chair, trying to shrink into his cubicle as much as he could. He would answer some questions about why a new television won't work (Have you tried plugging it in?), and exchange some chats with Charlie, another support operator that worked four cubicles down. Charlie was Jerold's best friend, but that was more due to the fact that he was his only friend, not a close bond between the two. They would eat lunch together around noon, with the conversation normally revolving around classic Bond movies, if there was a conversation at all. Jerold thought that Sean Connery portrayed 007 the best, but Charlie insisted that Roger Moore was better.

While conversations with Charlie were when Jerold was most relaxed, they weren't his favorite part of the day. His favorite part of the day was seeing Her. He didn't know her name, or anything about her in fact. What he did know was her smile, the way it shone and filled the whole floor with a radiant energy that kept him looking over at her, only to quickly avert his eyes if she even hinted at returning his gaze. She thrilled him and terrified him all at once. They had exchanged pleasantries once at the water-cooler, but the exchange of words was anything but pleasant for Jerold. He remembered the encounter vividly: His 360 turn to make sure the coast was clear for him to proceed to the cooler, the 13 quick steps it took him to get there, his eyes moving from his cup to the hallway, looking for signs of life as the water slowly filled, and then, Her. She came from nowhere, almost as if she had appeared out of thin air. In the 3 seconds that transpired between the time Jerold first saw her and her arrival at the water-cooler, his heart rate had doubled, and his mouth had become a dry pit.

"Hello," she said through a smile. "How are you?"

Jerold fumbled for the right words, struggling to make coherent thoughts. How was he? What was he supposed to say? Should he give her the truth, and offer up "Oh, I'm about to go into cardiac arrest if I can't get out of this conversation in the next twenty seconds?" Instead, after an especially long pause, he managed to squeak out "Fine, thanks." And then she was gone. All of that hard work, all of the strength it took for him to even produce a sound, and she just simply rounded the corner, onwards towards her destination. His face went red as he took a sip from his water.

Jerold was brought back to the present when a ping came through his computer speakers. He opened his Internet browser and saw an unopened chat. He clicked on it, expecting another mindless consumer to be asking a question that could easily be answered by reading the instructions. What he read, however, set off a sequence of events that changed his outlook on life forever.

It started with a message from his boss, asking Jerold to go downstairs and across the street to the Starbucks and bring back a black coffee for him, no cream. The request wasn't too out of the ordinary, as Jerold had done random tasks like these for him before. It didn't bother him, running errands, he liked being able to take time out of the office and keep to himself. He grabbed his jacket and headed for the stairs. When he opened the door, a rough looking man, perched on top of a ladder with a paintbrush in his hand, greeted him. "Stairs are closed. For emergencies only."

Jerold was stunned. He had hardly ever seen anyone in the stairwell, let alone spoken to someone. This was one of his sanctuaries, one of the places where he felt safest from others, and from himself. And now he was being told to leave? Sure, the off-white paint was peeling off the walls. The stairwell was a bleak ascension (or declension, depending on the way you were going) from point A to point B. Was it pretty? No. But it was a stairwell for crying out loud, not the Louvre.

"I...I just need... I'm trying to..."

"Look bud, if it's not an emergency, you need to go. There's some serious fumes in here right now." The man tapped the paper mask he wore around his mouth and nose.

"I'm only going down two floors." Jerold figured his only chance of making it past the painter was with a lie.

"I'm not interested in where you are going. If the building isn't on fire, then you need to take the elevator." It was clear to Jerold now that the handyman wasn't going to let him through.

With much disdain, he turned on his heel and headed back through the door and into his office floor. There were many things that Jerold didn't want to do that day. He didn't want to get shot or mugged, for example. That was never good. He didn't want step in dog crap, or have to walk through a dirty combination of snow and water. He quite liked his shoes. But the one thing that Jerold wanted no part of more than anything else was a twelve-story ride in an elevator.

186

After a brief mental deliberation, he decided to head back to his desk and try again later. He had only taken four steps when a voice stopped him dead in his tracks.

"Jerry, right?" Mr. Dalton, Jerold's boss, was standing by the elevator lobby. "Have you been down to the 'Buck yet?"

"Um, well no but I-"

"That's ok, I'm going down to eleven. You can go down with me." Almost as soon as Jerold's boss finished his sentence, the elevator doors opened. A robotic voice informed those within range that the machine was going down, and Mr. Dalton stepped onto the elevator and turned around. There was a brief moment where Jerold stood face-to-face with his boss, still standing in the lobby. Jerold took a deep breath and stepped into the machine from hell.

The elevator began its descent with a violent jolt, and Jerold felt his heart sink into his stomach. His head was spinning, not from any of the fumes he might have inhaled in the stairwell, but from nerves. He began to chew on his fingers like they were the only things he had eaten all day. Six seconds passed until the elevator came to a halt. The small screen centered above the doors indicated that they had reached the eleventh floor. The doors opened.

"Black coffee, no cream." Mr. Dalton said as he exited the elevator. "Make it a large too – And be quick."

Jerold watched as his boss turned a corner and

disappeared out of sight. He had called him Jerry, which was the closest he had been to Jerold. James, Jack, and Gary were other names that Mr. Dalton had called Jerold. After Mr. Dalton got off, Jerold was alone on the elevator. There was no one waiting in the eleventh floor lobby, and he knew that in four seconds the doors would close, and he would be left alone for at least another floor. He began the count in his head. One Mississippi. Nothing. Two Mississippi. No one. Three Mississippi. Safe. Four Mississippi. The doors began to close when a hand appeared between the cracks, forcing the door to reopen. Jerold slowly traced the hand back to its owner. It was Hers.

Startled, Jerold took a step back towards the corner of the elevator. He pulled on the collar of his jacket, wishing he could disappear into its soft, pillow-like folds. Of all the people that could have been on the bottom two floors. Why did it have to be Her?

"This is going down, right?" The question startled Jerold. He cursed internally. Why did she have to ask a question? A comment or greeting and he could have just nodded, gave a little grin and then sunk back into his personal cave. A question asked directly to him had to be answered.

"Yes, I think." Jerold felt his cheeks turn into rosebushes. He hoped that she wasn't going all the way to the ground floor, that he wouldn't have to sweat out another 10 floors. But another part of him, deep down inside, enjoyed her presence. She terrified him, of course. Yet she made him smile, not physically, but with his thoughts. She made him feel warm. Then again, that could have just been the jacket.

The elevator began to inch closer to the ground again, and She had yet to hit a button on the panel. The only button illuminated was the ground floor. Jerold watched the screen as the numbers fell slowly. Ten... Nine... Eight... Seven... Six. The elevator came screeching to a halt on the sixth floor. It shook and growled softly as the doors opened and two more people got onto the elevator. They would seem innocent enough to most people, both older gentleman dressed in suits, the man with the grey hair in a navy one, and the bald man in a black one. To Jerold, they were two people crowding in on him. Either one of them could easily try and strike up a conversation.

All was quiet as the elevator jolted into motion again. The two businessmen were standing shoulder-to-shoulder by the door. Jerold was standing in the back right corner, leaning into the wall with his elbow. She was standing just two feet to the left of him. The elevator was making a lot of noise as it passed the fifth floor, and then crashed to another stop at the fourth floor. The doors opened and a janitor quickly stepped inside, with the name "Reggie" sewn on in cursive on the right breast of his blue work uniform.

Jerold knew that he only needed to hold out for four more floors. What was that, fifteen seconds? He could do that, at least he hoped. The ride down had been as peaceful as it could be, all things considered. No one had talked since the two businessmen got on, but standing in a confined space with four other people gave Jerold a stomach of nerves. Of course, having Her standing only a couple of feet away from him didn't do much to help.

A horrible noise echoed throughout the elevator shaft as the machine began to move closer to sea level. Jerold could feel the elevator dropping, but the pace seemed slower than before. He kept an eye on the screen that displayed the floor – it hadn't moved since Reggie the janitor got on. He was looking at the screen when a horrendous noise came from outside of the elevator. It resonated throughout the interior of the elevator, and all of a sudden, they weren't moving. Everyone looked around at each other with worried eyes, not sure what to do. Jerold was distraught, though his physical exterior remained calm. Being on a moving elevator was bad enough. Being stuck with three strangers and the woman of his dreams in a 8 x 6 metal box? Jerold wasn't sure there was anything worse than that.

"What should we do?" The grey haired businessman spoke first. He turned his shoulders to face the back of the elevator, as did his bald headed associate. Now they were all standing in a circle, with Jerold still leaning as far into the corner as his body would let him.

"Hit the alarm button, should call the downstairs desk." Reggie the janitor offered the advice. After he did so, the bald headed man leaned over to he panel of buttons and pressed on the bell shaped alarm button. Almost as soon as he did so, the elevator shook and quickly dropped several feet before abruptly stopping again. This time though, the lights cut out.

And that's when it happened. It was quick, a flash of light in Jerold's soul when the physical lights around him went dark. She was still standing next to him, and when the elevator fell, she stumbled towards his direction. When the elevator went dark, she grabbed his hand. Jerold didn't flinch, didn't cower away from her soft, smooth fingers that wrapped delicately around his wrist. Here was a man that was too afraid of himself to even speak to others, to afraid of being shunned or cast away to a deserted island to present himself to the world. But in this moment, he was a security blanket. His presence, his existence was calming the worries of another person. And not just any person. Hers.

She quickly released her grip. If Jerold's eyes weren't in the process of adjusting to the dark, he would have noticed that her cheeks had morphed into rosebushes. Jerold let out a nervous laugh as she mumbled an apology.

As the other individuals in the elevator grumbled to themselves, Jerold took a moment to take in his surroundings. He was positioned in the back right corner of the lift, with Reggie the Janitor directly in front of him, the two business man in the front left of the elevator, and Her, only two feet to his left. The elevator felt a lot a more spacious when he was alone, but now that he shared its interior with four other people he began to feel cramped. He guessed that the lift was about four by eight feet, with each square foot of the floor being composed of white tiles. Wood paneling lined the lower third of the walls, while the rest of wall was made up of stainless steel. He could tell that whoever designed the elevator tried to make it look classy. It was about as classy as a tuxedo t-shirt.

"Well... What now?" The question came from the

bald businessman in the upper left corner of the elevator.

"I knew I should have waited for another elevator. Maintenance guys have been complainin' about this lift for weeks." Reggie the Janitor was speaking now. "This is the second time it's stuck itself in the last month."

"That's encouraging." The bald businessman replied. "Any idea how long we could be here for?"

"Usually don't take more than an hour or so." Reggie replied.

"Well then, we might as well get acquainted with one another if we are going to be here for a while." The bald man suggested. "My name's William, I'm an account downstairs for Barnum and Sheets."

"Richard Withers, I work with William on certain projects now and then." The grey haired man put his hands in his pockets and let out a sigh.

"Well as you can probably tell by my name tag here, name's Reggie, Reggie Crawford. I unclog toilets and tighten screws on desks and chairs." Reggie deadpanned, and after noticing the uneasy look he was getting, let out a laugh. "Hey, it pays alright."

As the men in the front of the elevator introduced themselves, Jerold's Heart began to race. The sense of calm that had washed over him when She had touched his hand had long since passed. If She were to grab his hand now, she would feel how sweaty and clammy his palms had become. Jerold knew there was no getting out of introducing himself. He was terrified. Yet he also knew that She would have to introduce herself as well, and for that, he was excited. Maybe, he thought, just maybe it would be worth it.

"I'm Jerold." Before he had realized what had happened, he had spoke. His eyes widened, and he suddenly became hyperaware of his situation. There was a pause before he started speaking again. "I work for support at NewTech, um, answering chats and stuff." He coughed and pushed back into the wall. Jerold wished he could snap his fingers and disappear. Maybe if he tried hard enough, he would be able to wake up from his nightmare.

A soft voice came from his left. "My name is Clarisse." Four words from Her, no not her, Clarisse, were all it took to calm his nerves. "I work with Jerold at NewTech, except I work as a secretary, just directing phone calls and such. So... is anyone being kept from anything important?"

Each occupant talked about what lead him or her to being on the elevator, and what the break down was keeping him or her from. Even Jerold offered a few sentences on how he was supposed to be back by now with a large black coffee for his boss.

He stumbled over some words, and didn't say too much, but he talked. He talked about himself, to strangers. If they hated him, ridiculed him, or rejected him, he had nowhere to go, nothing to fall back into. He even took off his jacket after the first 15 minutes. The dark helped him to relax. He couldn't see the details of anyone's faces, only the silhouettes that reminded him they were there at all. The only person he could see was Her. No, not Her... *Clarisse*.

He couldn't literally see her. It was almost pitch black in the elevator, as the emergency lights never came on. He could see a glint from her eyes, and her teeth were barely visible when she opened her mouth. But he could see her better than ever before, standing there in the dark. He knew that when she smiled, her nose crinkled just above the bridge. He knew her, period. He knew her name, knew her hobbies. He knew her background and her goals. He even asked her a direct question. It took him a solid 10 minutes to muster up the courage to do so, and when he finally did, it took all of his energy not to laugh at her response. Pierce Brosnan was Clarisse's favorite James Bond. Yuck. Jerold even told a joke once, though he couldn't remember what it was about. He didn't mean to tell it, it just spilled out of his mouth before he could zip himself shut. None of the men laughed, but he heard Clarisse snort a giggle. Quite frankly, that's all that really mattered to him.

When the elevator jolted back to life again, everyone gave a half-hearted cheer. Everyone except for Jerold. When Jerold got onto the elevator, all he wanted to do was get off. But when the time finally came for him to do so, he didn't want to go. He didn't want this moment to disappear.

They ended up stuck in the elevator for an hour. There was Reggie, the father of five from upstate New York who unclogged toilets and mopped floors, all day, every day to make a living. There was William, the bald headed accountant from the marketing firm that operated through the bottom 10 floors. Richard, his grey-haired associate, was 58 and beginning to flirt with retirement. He had a grandson who was in the second grade, and he desperately wanted to watch him play football while he was still young. Then there was Clarisse.

She was 22, a graphic designer working as a secretary who enjoyed movies and literature. She was a recent graduate of Kansas State University, and this was her first year living in the city. She wanted to explore the world, but couldn't afford it. So she came to the one place where the world was best represented. That's what New York City meant to her. All of the nationalities and people, all of the ideas and energy, she wanted to be a part of it. And here she was.

The lights never came back on in the elevator, so when the doors split open on the ground floor, the light blinded the group temporarily. One by one, everyone slowly exited the lift. First William and Richard, then Reggie. After Reggie, Clarisse stepped out, leaving Jerold alone in the elevator. He looked around, stunned that the conversations were over, that he was back by himself, where he so desperately wanted to be before the elevator got stuck. He shielded his eyes with his forearm and groggily stepped into the light. For the first time since telling the others, he remembered the whole reason he had come down to the lobby in the first place. Mr. Dalton would not be happy about his delayed coffee.

Jerold moved towards the doors of the building, intent on making it back with the coffee as quickly as he could. Before he could take three steps, a familiar soft hand tapped him on the shoulder.

"It was nice to finally learn you name, Jerold." Clarisse stood not two feet in front of him, looking directly into his eyes.

"Clarisse is a pretty name." Jerold smiled, and for a second he didn't worry about what anyone thought of him. He felt accepted. He felt safe.

There was a moment, after both individuals completed the others names. It didn't last long, only a second or two, while both of them looked into each other's eyes. Clarisse looked like she was waiting for something, waiting for Jerold to ask her something perhaps. When he didn't say anything, she just giggled and turned away.

"I'll see you around." Jerold said sheepishly as she walked off.

"Yes, you will." Clarisse gave him one last grin before disappearing into the city.

Bullshit Kickball Rules
Zack Peercy

So I know you're dead and you probably won't read this, but I thought it was important that you know something: We used to have ninth period PE together in seventh grade. That's not the something you should know, but more of a lead in. Sorry, I'll get to the something soon.

Do you remember playing kickball in gym class? There was that fucked up rule about being tagged out. If we kicked a fair ball, we could be tagged before reaching first. No one ever wanted to throw the ball to the first baseman. The gym class heroes prefered to peg outcasts like us directly on our respective runs. A ball to the chest or the face was the cherry on top of our inadequacies.

If that hadn't been a rule, maybe the first baseman wouldn't have caught the ball or an anti-social outfielder would have throw it the wrong way. And then we'd be safe on base hoping the bell would ring and end the day's torture. But as you bunted the ball with the side of your foot and that pizza-faced pitcher with a buzz cut scooped up the ball, I saw that damn rule implemented when the ball made contact with the side of your face.

On my way home, I was nursing a fresh stomach welt from class when I saw you walking ahead of me with your friend. I didn't want to pass you because I knew your friend hasn't liked me since fifth grade when I assumed he was gay due to a Jonas Brothers obsession

197

and a lisp. He turned out to actually be gay. I'm not sure if that retroactively removes my homophobia; probably not.

Anyway, it was really hot for early April, but I still wore my green army jacket with the wool lining because it made my body look more proportional. You wore a red polo and khaki pants that represented everything really well. You always looked nice despite limiting dress code. I always looked like I needed a shower. Your dark hair hung down and swayed as you walked, showing glimpses of your pale neck and Hot Topic jewelry.

Despite the reasonable distance, I could hear your voice. You talked about joining drama club in high school. Given your projection skills, I thought you would be center stage for every show with a spotlight operated by yours truly during your solos.

It got to the point where I either had to pass you or start a conversation. The latter I would never attempt due to clammy hands and a protruding gut, so I went to pass you on your left. It was uphill and my brief kickball participation still had me winded, so it took a little too long and involved a little too much heavy breathing.

I know that we've had small social interactions in the past, but this is the only one I vividly remember. You turned and looked at me, and, although I felt the warmth of your gaze, I avoided eye contact because I was afraid of your judgement. You looked down and said, "I like your shoes."

They were a pair of white limited edition Grateful Dead Converse hi-tops. Jerry Garcia, a name I only held synonymous with ice cream, designed the hippie skeleton imprinted on the side. The overpriced sneaker got an approving nod from the Future Burnouts of America I called friends. They were a pair of shoes that were too narrow for my foot, that people purposely stepped on because they were white, that people made fun of because of the way they wrapped around my cankles; you said you liked them.

And I ignored you. I walked right past you, I tried not to hear your friend call me a freak, and I went home.

It would have been really easy for me to just say, "thank you." I could have started a conversation, or a friendship, or a relationship, but I didn't. And that was so rude of me.

So I just wanted to say that I didn't deserve your compliment. And you didn't deserve cancer.

I left that school a year later because transferring is one of the many perks of being poor. This demoted our status as passerby to total strangers. At the time, I was fine leaving because I hated almost everyone. You were barely a memory to me until I heard about your diagnosis. Your compliment rattled around in my head all that day and every day since.

You died after your senior year, making high school, a time when you're surrounded by, let's face it, a bunch of assholes, the best years of your life. You left an impact on the town you left behind. Years later, people still wish you a post-mortem happy birthday. You still inspire people to do great things because you can do nothing.

And it's awful that you're adored, and it sucks that

you're prayed for, and it's bullshit that you have to be remembered for who you were. Because you could have been so much more. You just got tagged out too early.

How to Cope Using Similes
Zack Peercy

My life before you was like
having a cold;
girls avoided me
in fear of viral infection,
and a ton of used Kleenex
lay crumpled on my floor.

Meeting you was like
smelling home after a trip abroad;
dusty rose petals and Swedish Fish
blended to create a familiarity
I wish I had
recognized sooner.

Talking to you was like
waterboarding a lemur;
your eyes stretched wide,
bursting with anxiety,
as bits of conversation
slowly dripped out.

Going out with you was like
being a rookie astronaut;
exhilarating weightlessness
on my first mission
exploring a small isolated moon
with a well-traveled surface.

Hearing you say, "I love you" was like
critiquing porn stars;
"great vocalization

with a nice build up
to the money shot,
but lacking substance."

Fucking you was like
feeding my guinea pig;
unwanted biting
and entitled squeaks
as I tell myself, "I'll eat later"
and, "at least she's fed."

Asking you for support was like
decorating an office cubicle;
short term pacifiers,
loosely tacked on cardboard walls,
with cliche expressions like,
"Well, it could be worse!"

Being there for you was like
inspecting the Pyramids;
trying to navigate dim corridors
and interpret a symbol's meaning
while avoiding booby-traps
purposefully set to bring my end.

Arguing with you was like
investigating a serial killer;
long ordeals --drawn out
by incompetence and no
comprehension of intent--
that remained unresolved.

You breaking up with me was like
meeting an estranged parent;
spewing this bullshit
like, "you never needed me

to become a great person"
to make yourself feel better.

Getting over you has been like
having a shark bite off my arm;
still feeling your phantasm
but having a fucking sweet
solar powered robotic prosthetic
that can probably shoot lasers.

Weeping Woman
Elizabeth Loch

I entered the cottage
Reeking of fish,
Where the weeping woman sits
At a cold, unfriendly hearth.

Dear madam, said I,
Tell us why you mourn
And are so forlorn.

I am not a madam, said she,
But a sister of earth and air
My people are proud and fair—
And her eyes were far away.

You are of the folk, cried I,
Who steal children and young brides
You who in the moonlight ride.

I am not, she shook her flaming hair,
I cry for those out of time
And will soon sleep in grime—
And tears flooded her eyes.

Jesus, a Junk Drawer
Jordan Carter

Three silver shots
split through
the singlewide
metal
clink on
metal
it sounded like
it would be
hot
His mother
standing there
hands
shaking and no one
to touch her

And he ran

He wondered
what it would be
like to have a spare
bedroom
Jesus
a junk drawer

dont ring the bell
dont knock
you know the drill
come now

205

and come quick

Instead he had
bare feet
an empty
package of Ora-Jel
a bag of deer guts
the sky bored and blue

The Wild Thing Running Down the Hill

Jordan Carter

For Miles

Cyclobenzaprine 5 mg
Take one tablet by mouth three times a day as needed
for muscle spasms

You kept pill bottles as film canisters
in your bedroom and I
slept in the last bed you slept in
last night

It was almost like old times—
going over to your green and yellow house
sitting with your parents and waiting
for you to come home
from the skate park

but you never do

I looked for you in every room
in every silver vase—
looked for a kid strung out on summer
adrenaline kick flip heat

I touched your ashes, bone white, ghost white
They're like pulverized seashells
held inside a bag

I think you'd think it funny
that all of you can fit

in that. Your brain somewhere, your eyes, your teeth.
Your mother

left you on the couch with me
along with the pair of grey corduroys you were wearing
$1.37 in the pocket

I sat with you a minute in that house on Front Street
and then I picked you up and put you back
where you belong
on the bottom shelf of a bookcase

I did not cry
because that is not you

You are the rash on my arms
the books on my shelf
the zine on my fridge.

Whales and You

Jordan Carter

i am seven and perfect
He tells me, just what He wants
because i am hairless
clean
because my Mother still washes me
lifts the hair at the nape of my neck and rings
a washcloth over my head into the water
because i smell like baby oil
and can't come yet

when Mom is gone we play
Hide Inside and Don't Squeak

He leaves His socks on

i am fourteen and imperfect
too old for Him, hairy and dirty
and i come too quick

but He still leaves His socks on
and presses my cheek into the carpet

from here
it looks like the whales on my wallpaper
are surfacing

209

Epitome of Awkward
Bethany Wicks

The weight on my shoulders makes me feel like a turtle with my entire house on my back. I need to find a place to sit before my legs give out the only problem being that the library is surprisingly full for a Friday night. For God's sake, I wouldn't even be here if it weren't for my roommate kicking me out so he could screw his girlfriend. And while I appreciate the warning, I don't really enjoy being kicked out of my own room.

"Whatever," I think to myself as I bound up to the next floor in search of a chair. The third floor is split into three different parts: books shelves, computers, and a lounge. The lounge is full of mismatching tables and chairs that look like they came from a crappy garage sale. My footsteps echo on the wood floor, making everyone look up at me with unpleasant eyes. Normally I'd probably care, but I found a couch to sit on and that's all I care about. Once I reach the couch, I slide my backpack off my shoulder until it slips and thuds to the ground causing everyone to glare at me again. I mentally give them all the finger and sit down on the couch.

"What the actual shit!" someone mutters angrily. I look over my laptop screen to see the speaker, a girl sitting reading a book in the armchair across from me. I smile when I spot her because she is just the epitome of awkward.

She's sitting sideways in the chair so that her legs are draped over the arm in a way that seems very uncomfortable. One of her hands is in her red hair bunching it up in different directions, killing any sort of order. She's glaring at the book and flipping the pages so intensely that I'm afraid she's going to rip the next one. Sure enough, two pages later she rips the corner.

"Damnit," she curses probably not realizing how loud she is.

"Shhh," the librarian hisses at her with a disapproving look before walking away. The girl looks up from the book and glares at the librarian as if she has just done the worst thing possible. When the glaring ends she swings her legs over so she's sitting in a normal fashion and grabs her bag from the floor. She rifles through it for a while, dumping the contents on the table in front of her. At first, it's normal objects like notebooks, folders, and highlighters, but then she starts pulling out things like rainbow sharpies, crayons, and playdough. A few things roll off the table and skitter across the floor creating an even bigger mess that she doesn't even acknowledge. Finally, she smiles and pulls out a roll of tape.

I know I should be doing homework or something productive, but she's just interesting to watch. I'm aware of how creepy this sounds but she's like a beautiful trainwreck I can't look away from. I like that I know her hair is dyed, but it looks natural on her. She's wearing a hoodie, but she still looks pretty in an unconventional way. She's strange but intriguing all at the same time, and everything she does makes me what to know more about her. Who is this girl?

***

"Hey Riley, uh you mind?" Steve says from the doorway where he's standing there with his arm tight around his girlfriend Kathrine. Steve is the big bulky football type of guy, and sometimes I swear he's just as dense. His girlfriend, on the other hand, is a stunning contrast. I'm sure Kathrine is smart and makes good choices but when it comes to being with Steve, she's a total floozy, hanging on him like mold on a shower curtain. I give it a week.

"Could you, uh, go for a walk or something?" Steve stammers again while Katherine nibbles on his ear.

"Seriously?" I say, not hiding the anger in my voice. "This is my room too, ya know." I'm pretty sure Steve isn't even pretending to listen anymore because now he's just mumbling and returning Katherine's sloppy kisses. "Jesus Christ, you need a hobby!"

"We have a hobby." Steve looks away from Katherine for just long enough to wink creepily and shut the door with his foot. Apparently this party was moving to the bed quickly and clearly I wasn't invited.

"Fine, I'll go do laundry..." My voice trails off as I realize no one is listening to me. Grumbling to myself I put down the book I was reading and jump off my bed. I grab my backpack, laundry soap, and my basket and head towards the door. "Oh and fucking like rabbits isn't a hobby," I shout back at them before slamming the door. A few people in the hallway look towards me with confused and judging glaces.

I sigh and make my way to the elevator.The entire way down to the basement I'm thinking about relationships and sex and how they're really not the same thing. For instance, you can have sex without having a relationship but rarely do you find a relationship without sex. Out of nowhere the red head from the library pops into my head and my face gets hot.

The elevator door opens revealing a basement that resembles the opening scene of a low budget horror film, complete with dirty floors, flickering lights, and a strange smell. Maybe this really is a horror movie and I'm about to die brutally? I look over my shoulder, shrug and continue down the hallway.

From here I can hear someone in the laundry room talking, or wait maybe they're singing? Yeah, there's definitely a girl singing in there. Suddenly I feel strange just walking in there and interrupting, but then again I don't have anywhere else to go.

I walk in to find four of the five washers are filled and spinning, empty laundry baskets littering the floor, and most interestingly there's the redhead girl lying on top of the washers singing "Revolution" by The Beatles. The girl's eyes are closed, her hands behind her head, and tapping her foot to the beat she's singing. Her voice is somewhere between caterwauling and acceptable.

Unsure of what to do, I walk over to the other side of the room and put down my stuff on the table as quietly as possible so not to disturb her. There's supposed to be chairs to go with the table over here but for some reason, they're missing, probably taken by some drunken idiot. I decided to hop up and sit on the table.

So far the girl hasn't acknowledged my existence due to the big aqua headphones wrapped around her head. I smile, pull out my book, and continue reading, all the while listening to the girl switch to another Beatles song.

After about twenty minutes and fifty pages, the girl has moved on to a song I don't recognize. The lyrics are strange and the register has changed into something the girl can actually sing quite well. I can tell the girl really enjoys The Beatles but in all honesty, she doesn't have the voice for it, whatever this song is suits her better.

One of the washers the girl is on buzzes loudly cutting her off mid-sentence. I continue reading, waiting for

214

the girl to continue with the rest of the song. When the room stays quite after a moment, I look up to find the girl sitting up hugging her knees to her chest.

"Uhhhhhhh...." She mumbles pulling her knees closer to her as if trying to make herself invisible. I rack my brain trying to think of something to say that will make her feel better. What would Steve say? Oh god no, I shouldn't say that...what about...

"You have a really nice voice," I say stumbling and stammering over my own words. This seems to catch her off guard, making her cheeks blush a rosy pink and loosen the vise-like grip on her legs. I smile back at her unaware of what else to do. The girls eyes wander around the room finally resting on my laundry basket.

"Why didn't you, uh, I don't know, do your laundry?" The girl laughs slightly and I think she has finally relaxed.

"I didn't want to disturb you..." I shrug.

"I'm Nikki," she states after a moment of awkward silence.

"Riley," I tell her. She smiles, hops off the washer, and starts walking towards me. "What are you doing?" I ask her. Nikki is picking up my basket and walking over to the line of washers. I jump off the table and follow her over unsure of what else to do.

"Here, take my washer," she looks over her shoulder and smiles at me. For a moment, I'm so caught up in her smile that I forget she's talking to me. "Hello? Earth to Riley?" She laughs, snapping her fingers in my face.

"What'd you say?" I ask, mentally hitting myself in the face for sounding like an idiot. Oh god, maybe Steve is rubbing off on me.

"I said you could take my washer, I'm done with it." She says placing my basket on top of the washer and begins emptying it of it contains.

 "So Riley?" Nikki asks voice muffled by the washer. "Do you always stalk girls in the laundry room or is this just a special Tuesday night?"

The Cough
Kayla Nelson

Daniel was wrong. Just within the week the first victim of Marburg had been taken in America. Some third world countries were starting to execute anyone who contracted the disease. Families went into hiding to keep loved ones safe from death, only for them all to die together from the virus. Victims of this disease were not to meet a happy end. It would start out simple with a cough or sneezing. Which would grow into a fever. After the beginning stage vomiting and diarrhea would occur. The victim's eyes would grow blood shot. But the worst part, was the internal bleeding. Every major organ in their bodies would start to bleed out, causing bleeding to come from the eyes, and any other exit from the body. This disease alone had already claimed over 1000 lives and it was still growing.

It was spreading too fast for researchers to handle. They couldn't study it because anyone who contradicted it would die within ten days. No time at all to study the infection itself without risking getting infected their selves. Schools started to close down, the ones who carried the virus were quarantined in their own homes, and families were pulled apart from each other.

 Now with over 2000 known cases of Marburg in America the Johnson family took distract measures to protect themselves from the disease. Daniel took his

217

family, some food, and a few emergency weapons down into their cellar. With no windows, and he would board up and seal the only exit shut, they would be safe from the horrible fate outside. Diana brought her phone and charger down to keep tabs on the outside world as they huddled together in their dark hole.

Cindy and Brandon were easy to distract themselves with their little games, minds still innocent at the age of seven, Diana was still texting away on her phone but Daniel and Maria were worried senseless. What if this wasn't enough? And someone would get sick anyway? Would they kill the family member before they caught it? Better one death than five.

Brandon had brought his little bird friend, who had saved a week prior with a broken wing, down with him. The wing of the bird was getting better and it was chirping more now since it was healing properly. His mother, Maria told him that the birds wing would fully heal in two weeks. Most of the time, the family spent their hours in silence. The only light they had was the flash light Daniel had brought down and the dim glow coming off Diana's phone.

Hours turned into days as the family continued their time in silence in the hole. Even America had stooped to the point of killing people before the virus could spread even more. Bodies were piling up in the grave yards as the virus claimed more and more victims in its gruesome hold.

It was then in the pitch black room.

Somebody coughed.

Daniel was the first to look up and flicked on the light. The shadows escaping back to the corners of the room to flee from the glow. "Who was it?"

Nobody spoke up. Maria sat beside her husband, Cindy and Brandon were curled up in each other's arms, and Diana clutched her phone close to her chest.

"I said, who was it?!" Daniel's voice grew harder as he shined his light onto each member of the family's faces. Diana had tears in her eyes, not sure if it was from their current situation or if she was now worried for her own life.

No one spoke, they only looked to each other in silence. Eyes gazing up and down at everyone to see who would admit to the cough.

"It wasn't us," Brandon said for both he and Cindy.

"It wasn't me," Diana said with a shrug.

"I know I didn't cough," Maria said to her husband.

"Well it sure as hell wasn't me," Daniel huffed out to their denials. "It had to be somebody so why don't you just admit who it was and take your fate."

Yet again nobody spoke up. No one wanted to accept their fate of death so quickly. Even though they were going to die anyway, they still had a 12% of living with the virus rather than the 0% chance of admitting it to the people around them.

The time seemed to last forever in silence as no one

admitted to the crime of the cough. The only sound was the bird chirping occasionally and the heart beats in their chest.

"Coughing is the first sign of the virus! Somebody needs to own up to it!" The father said with a stern gruff as he stood from the ground.

"Can't we just wait to see if it was just dust?" Maria asked her husband.

"Honey, you see what is going on out there! They are killing people at the first sign of the virus! It's one or all."

Maria hung her head and looked to each one of her children. "Well I'm telling you it wasn't me." Her voice held a venom to it as her eyes pierced her husband.

"It wasn't me!" Diana said as she stood from the ground as well. "But I know I won't die from this virus so one of you better speak up right now!"

The time in silence had taken a toll on the family. In a survival situations the mind does weird things to keep itself alive. Humans could eat other humans, murders happen to survive, and this case was no different. All though they were family, it was better to sacrifice one life for the greater good than to let them all die.

"It was Cindy!" Brandon said suddenly as he pushed his sister away from her.

"No it wasn't! He is lying! I didn't cough!" The little blonde girl cried out.

Daniel walked over and picked up the girl from the

ground, "Cindy tell daddy right now. Did you cough?" He ended each word to add emphasize.

The little girl held tears in her eyes and she began to scream out that it wasn't her that coughed. But how could anyone tell if she was telling the truth or lying? Children lie all the time to save themselves from getting punished, surely they would lie to save themselves from being killed.

Maria jumped up and pulled her daughter away from the man's hold. "Don't you dare touch my baby," she shrieked to the man.

"If she coughed we have to kill her!" He yelled pointing a finger to the girl.

"How do we know you didn't cough?" Diana challenged her father.

"Because it wasn't me!"

"But how do we know that? You could have coughed but are lying to save your own skin!"

"You will not talk to me like that young lady! I am your father and you will obey me!"

"You are my father but if you coughed then you can't be pointing a gun at anyone else."

The man sneered at the girl and back handed her onto the ground again. Cindy was still crying but Maria jumped up and grabbed the gun from her husband and pointed it at him. "Diana has a point. How do we know it wasn't you that coughed? You keep accusing everyone else, how do we know it wasn't you?"

The father turned around with his flash light in hand to face his armed wife. "So if it was me then what? You shoot me and then someone coughs again if it wasn't me and then you just killed an innocent man."

Silence rang throughout the room again, no one was sure of what to do. Cindy was still sniffling and Brandon held his baby bird box close to him. Diana hid in the corner having her phone turned off trying to just stay hidden.

"Look, let's just wait again and see if someone coughs again," Daniel now agreed to his wife's plan with the gun pointed at him now.

"No! You said so yourself it's one or all." Maria used her own husbands words against him as she kept the gun steadily pointed at him.

"You can't kill me, Maria. You don't have the strength to pull the trigger."

The wife was silent, only the air coming from her nose could be heard as she eyed where her husband stood. "Turn that light off and sit back down."

The husband gave a smirk and turned the light off. Filling the room in pitch black again.

Somebody coughed.

Daniel flipped the light back on and grabbed the gun away from his wife. "It was Brandon or Cindy!" He accused the two kids because he thought the cough came from that direction.

The youngest children huddle together in fear but this

time Cindy turned on Brandon claiming it was he who committed the crime. Of course the boy denied the claims made against him. This time was Cindy lying and saying it was Brandon to save herself or was she telling the truth. The father glared down at his children and then gave a heavy sigh. "I'm sorry kids."

Right before Maria could run over and stop him, he shot both children in the heads. Their small and fragile bodies fell over onto the ground, slumped together in a pile. Maria and Diana both screamed seeing the youngest children be the first to go.

"How could you." Maria screamed at her murderous husband. "They were so young!"

"Dammit Maria! I told you. It's one or all. Now they were going to die anyway so I just saved them that death!"

"You are a murderer! How do we know it was them who coughed?" Maria punched her husband sending the flash light over into a corner away from the three left standing.

Somebody coughed.

Maria looked over to her oldest daughter with wide eyes and frazzled hair. Diana shook her head and backed away from her mom.

"It wasn't me! It was dad!" The daughter denied the cough.

The dad of course denied it as well as he ran to get the flash light and pointed it at his wife, who's eyes were now blood shot. The coughing was starting to drive them mad. Survival was key and now with two children dead and the coughing still happening who was it.

"See! You killed my babies and it wasn't even them that coughed," Maria screamed at her husband. "You murderer!" She lunged at him with her nails digging into his face as she tried to beat him down.

Diana screamed seeing her mother turn primal against her father. The flash light and gun leaped from the man's hold as his was pinned against a wall. The ravenous Maria snarled and clawed at her husband constantly screaming out murderer. In defense, Daniel reached down and punched the woman in her gut over and over to make her get off him. Wild eyes and crazed hair, Maria bit down on her husband's neck making him bleed before he kicked her down on to the ground again. He jumped up and ran over to grab the gun which had fallen from his grasp. He picked it up and Maria stood up slowly with a laugh. He aimed the gun at her and as she lunged, he shot.

The teenager was now crying having seen her father kill both her mother and her siblings. Tears streamed down her face, her eyes blood shot as well now. Daniel breathed heavily, his shoulder rising and falling in beat with his breaths.

Just then, he let out a cough.

It was him all along who was coughing, which is why he was killing everyone else to save his own skin. Diana looked over and saw a rope, she knew her father was going insane and if she didn't do anything to stop this he would end up killing her too. Her fingers wrapped around the rope and while the man was distracted.

She jumped toward the man and wrapped the rope around his neck. The larger man thrashed about trying to shake the girl off of him. But she held on tight. Like a cow boy riding a bull, Daniel continued to run around the room beating the girl into the wall or trying to throw her over his back.

"You murderer! It was you all along!" The distraught teenager yelled as she held on through her tears. "You killed them! You killed them!"

"I did what I had to!" The man gasped trying to find his breath behind the rope around his neck.

The man slumped down against a wall with Diana behind him. His head thrashed trying to hit hers to get her to let go. His attempts were useless as she hid behind his back to avoid the head thrashing.

Daniel eyed the hand gun beside him and reached out in a final attempt. His fingers laced around the hold before turning the gun on his daughter behind him.

One shot rang out as it missed its target. The man felt light headed and the room around him began to spin. Diana screamed murderer over again as she fought to kill the man who killed her family.

A final chance. Daniel turned the gun behind him and pulled the trigger. The bullet met its mark but Diana still held on for a little longer.

Her grip loosened but it was too late for Daniel. His head rolled to the side in defeat and his body slumped down. Diana pushed him off her as tears cascaded her cheeks. Blood oozed from her side and her breaths caught in her throat.

The bird was now squawking from the all the commotion, desperately trying to get away. Diana crawled over to the bird and gingerly removed the bandage from its wing. The baby bird flew up into the air and with one smile, Diana closed her eyes as the bullet took its final life.

Lost

Jess Reed

Where do plans go
when put aside?
Do they sit, waiting
like books on a shelf?
Or fade—
falling to rags
Do they rot to pieces?
Or age like wine?
Probably they're tucked away
in a drawer
Kept safe
like Christmas ornaments
in July

Self Portrait as a Critic, a Mailman
Jess Reed

A doorbell now hangs by threadbare copper
smoke and tar leaks from windowpanes
The front door is unlocked
it always has been

I'll just leave it
the bundle of manila slips banded in a stack
some yellow, some pink, some green
all pastels

Pale black letters adorn the walls
"The mind of non-striking strikes!"
Nothing ever changes
Nothing

Death of a Composer
Jess Reed

Romantics of a lofty generation
Drunken beggars, pimps, madmen abound
Death of a vagrant, a dove

cholera sepsis poison cirrhosis suicide insanity
shaving bees mushrooms bicycles umbrellas
bookshelves
weak hearts, bad eyes
syphilis, syphilis, syphilis

Dusty Gods of a bygone era
preserved today,
for the dull and bored

Fishing Trip
Jess Reed

"Reel! Reel! Reel!"

That's not how it started, but that is the best part of
the story. Well, at least I think so. Most people would
probably agree once they've heard the whole thing, all
the way through, front to back. At least that's how it's
supposed to be, right? There are only two real,
necessary rules to any honest to goodness fishing story,
right? First, there is the exaggeration. You know, like
that time you caught something that technically
classifies as a minnow in the city pond, but the next
time you see your buddies it has developed into the
battle of a lifetime. You hold your hands three or four
feet apart and throw in a, "Man, you should'a seen that
thing!" as an extra touch. The second part is the climax,
the pitched battle between man and beast. Just where
the wave of narrative crashes and primitive brawn
vanquishes primordial instinct. Here, the fish comes
bursting from the depths to break the surface in
surrender. Disinterested, the men wipe their brows and
crack their beers, for it is they who have won the day.
At least, that's how it's supposed to go. My story is a
little different. It would probably help if I started at the
beginning, so let me take you back for just a second
and we will get things sorted out.

****

Our fishing story -- or is it a tale? I'll leave that up to
you, the reader -- begins with an innocent enough
question.

"Hey bud, do you want to go fishing?"

After the initial shock of the question, my mind was flooded with questions. Why now? Is this some kind of trap? Is this an intervention? Why is my Dad staging my intervention? Aren't interventions supposed to be a surprise? Will I need to RSVP my own intervention?

"Sure Dad." I said, wary of what he was going to say next.

"Great, we leave October 5th for the Inlet!"

Just like that, it was done. I had just agreed to a nine-hour road trip that would more than likely end with me vomiting over the side of a fishing vessel. In that moment, I envied those with crippling substance addictions -- they at least had an excuse. Me, though, I didn't even have the slightest drinking problem, let alone some full-blown ace-in-the-hole hard drug problem. Don't get me wrong. I wanted nothing more than to spend time with my dad, just not on a moving platform in the middle of the ocean.

So the day came, October 5th. I stood in the driveway next to my dad, half asleep, and wondered when I would be given my fishing pole. A truck turned the corner, rolled up the road, and came to a stop in front of us.

"You ready?" said an expectant voice as men began pouring out of the vehicle.

My dad grabbed our bags and threw them under the truck bed cover, "Yeeah"

"You'll have to sit middle since you'll fit," said the driver with a laugh. I climbed in and   realized that the middle "seat" was more than likely meant for a few grocery bags or a small dog, not for a 16 year old boy with legs. I made do. With my ass on a bench seat

and knees smashed into the stereo, we started our journey.

It was dusk before we reached our destination, and I still knew nobody's name except for Tom, who is my dad. Conversation in the truck consisted of fishing stories, work stories, wife stories, and the occasional beer story; all classics. We pulled into a shabby looking motel parking lot and parked underneath a giant faded aluminum sign that read "Sea Foam Motel." For good measure, the sign had been painted sea foam green. Crawling out of the truck, I waited for the blood flow to reach my legs so I could take a look around. I heard the ocean somewhere close and felt the fresh salt water air blowing all around me.

"Wait here, I'll grab the room keys and then we'll go eat," said the driver. Off he went,   out of the dim lighting of the parking lot and into the dusk. Within a few minutes, he   was back with a handful of keys.

"The restaurant's over behind our rooms on the other side of the motel. Hope you like seafood."

The restaurant, well...the restaurant looked like a water-damaged lean-to with a buffet shoved in the corner. I piled chunks of what looked like seafood onto my plate. Some things in shells, others not, all of it soaked in full sticks of butter. Back at the table, I looked around at the four men, Tom included. Each one of them looked as if they had served on a fishing barge in the South Pacific, in the 1970s. 'Yes, one of these men had been inside an opium den,' I assured myself, looking over the boiled pot of mess on the table in front of me.

"So you're Jess, huh? I'm Mike."

"And I'm Joe."

"Bill, nice to meet you."

Was it really that simple? After 10 hours together, it just came out? These three names, hid no romance or mystery. They were more like the names of men who would punch you in the mouth at the slightest provocation. These were men who knew their way around a wrench. I looked them over. Joe was a short man of about 50 with a leathery red tan, bristling grey facial hair all the way down to the eyebrows, and a small pair of readers. Mike looked much the same, only a bit slimmer with a facial expression that seemed to say, "I'll kick your ass." I decided I would do my best to stay clear of Mike. Bill was the only one of the three over 6ft tall. He was somewhere around 6'6", in fact. He had a military buzz-cut and could have easily been a high school football coach. All and all, it wasn't a bad group, albeit mildly frightening. I introduced myself.

"So you ready to fish?" asked Joe.

I assured him I was, in fact, born ready.

****

Waking up at 4am is something only sadists and

madmen should ever intentionally do. Yet, there I was, standing in the parking lot in pitch black, wondering if I'd ever get my fishing pole. The warm ocean breeze had turned to a chill only present in the later months of the year. I climbed into the truck, wedged into my seat and immediately fell asleep.

"Hey, wake up. You're gonna miss all the fishing," said someone, somewhere around   me.

Opening my eyes, I saw that everyone was standing outside the truck, and we were at a large inlet rimmed with long pier-like boat docks. I climbed out and was handed a penny.

"Flip on three, we'll keep going until we have the last man in the pole rotation."

'Pole rotation? Is there only one pole' I thought to myself.

What the hell kind of fishing trip is this? I threw my penny up anyhow and immediately lost it in the dark. Looking around, I saw everyone staring at me, pennies clamped on wrists, waiting. I bent down and started digging through the dim sandy grass.

"Heads," I said, dejected.

"You're out," said Mike.

This process kept going until we had our order. Joe, Tom, Mike, Bill, then Jess. Half an hour later, our captain and first mate arrived and introduced us to our boat, the Pelican. By that time, I was covered in mosquito bites from head to toe and glad to get inside the cabin. From what I could tell, the Pelican was a typical fishing boat. A closed cabin led up to the captain's chair. Behind the cabin was an open deck with a reeling chair mounted in the middle. For the next three and a half hours, we hummed out into the darkness. I laid on part of the cabin seat and dozed off.

As the sun pushed up past the horizon to show itself in full, the Pelican's engines kicked to a halt, and we began to coast through the water.

"Let's get some lines out!" yelled Arch, the captain.

Arch was less of a captain and more of a drill sergeant in cargo shorts. I scrambled for the deck. Finally, I saw the deck layout. We were not sharing a pole, and these were no ordinary poles either. There were nine massive fishing poles lining the deck, each slipped through a hole in the base of the boat. The idea was to pass the poles up to Arch, who would cast them for hundreds of yards around the boat. Rigging strung along the boat flanks dangled plastic fishing bait across the water's surface. Not soon after Arch threw out the last line, we got our first bite, then another, then another.

"Get those fucking poles in godammit!" yelled Arch.

'Didn't we just cast these?' I thought as I reeled in an empty pole in complete and utter terror. The idea, I later learned, was to get the empty poles out of the way of those with fish on them as fast as possible. I scrambled across the deck, grabbing pole after pole, reeled under men as they cursing fish and yanked lines. Spinning hooks flew from the water as giant empty poles bobbed up and over the cabin. Arch grabbed them all while steering blind with one hand, casting in intervals with the other. Three of four got their fish in, and the bites stopped.

"You're up next, Jess," said Joe.

Oh shit.

No sooner had he said it than the line bounced and a dolphin fish flew up out of the water, line in tow.

"Get the line! Grab it!" somebody screamed.

Suddenly I was holding a pole, and it was pulling back. One jump. Two Jumps. The dolphin launched from the water and up towards the boat followed by a Marlin. The Marlin exploded full from the water and caught the dolphin fish whole in midair.

"Reel! Reel! Reel!"

Thrashing, the Marlin smashed back into the water and took off.

"Back'er up!"

Somebody grabbed me around the waist and strapped on a belt to secure the pole. The boat, which had been slowly coasting, now tore through the water in bursts. First forward, the line yanked. Next back, the engines whined and plumes of black smoke poured up over the stern. The fish was too strong. Arch was backing full tilt to catch up with it while I wound the slack. Forward again.

"Reel! Pull it high!"

I wasn't reeling anymore; I was cranking the pole, up, down, up, down, up, down, one inch of line at a time.

"Back! Back it up Arch!"

I reeled until my arms hurt. I reeled for what felt like forever. I reeled until I didn't care anymore. I reeled on and on. The first mate slid across fresh fish blood and seawater coating the open deck and threw out his gaff pole. Then, suddenly there it was.

"Got'er!"

A ten-foot Marlin, glistening green and blue out across the water. One eye surfaced -- peering up, unblinkingly to the deck, and just like that she was gone. The catch was marked, and she was let go.

"Arch, that's gotta be a 500lb'er at least," said the first mate, who's name I never got.

And that is my fishing story.

Handlebars

Jess Reed

"He's sweeping the deck again," grinning, Becky let out a sigh. "That's the forth time today."

Out on the back deck stood a man crutched overtop a broom, knees bent. Back arched, he diligently gathered fallen leaves with jerking strokes, back and forth. Turning to face the patio door, he pressed on, head down all the while. He did not seem to notice, let alone acknowledge, those of us standing inside the living room.

A leather slipcase and notebook tucked into his flannel shirt pocket sagged as he turned round and round in search of the mess never fully gathered. Readers outlined his wrinkled face and slicked back greyed hairline. His name was Carl, and he looked every bit a product of the fifties left to age into the present day.

The thing was, he could not tell you exactly what the present day was.

The slipcase contained his wallet so it would not be lost, again. The notebook, scraps of information- the year, his name and birthday, dates of events long since passed. Carl had Alzheimer's. For lack of a better phrase, he was stuck, everyday a dimming mirror of the last. No longer made for the future, nor able to fully recount the past.

I walk out onto the deck and take a seat. "Well howdy," he says, still sweeping at nothing across the carpet. "I've been meaning to talk to you about something."

He sets the broom aside with the shaky strength of a man physically strong but mentally unsure. "How was Germany when you were there? I'm asking because when I was there with the Army, there was a whole lot of people not doing so good."

More or less, I tell him it was nice. To me, it is a reminder, the fifth time or so that I've told him about the changes in Europe over the past 65 years. Every time, the story gets a bit more watered down, a bit simpler. To him, it is something new, something fresh and relieving, knowing that those people over there are doing better. "Good, good." He wrings his hands and chews at nothing slowly. "That's good."

***

I watch him as he eats dinner. With a fork and knife, he scrapes a burger apart bit by bit. He does not talk. He does not look up. He is focused.

I wonder what it's like. To always be muddled, slowly set adrift and forever after lost at sea. Like being blind? Not seeing black, but seeing nothing. Unseeing. A waking dream of constant haze and disjointed, unexplainable events. Something incomprehensible to anyone but the afflicted. Untranslatable and unexplainable, a rift that can never be bridged by anyone or anything, least of all yourself.

"Carl, your mustache is looking exquisite today." says his granddaughter from across the table, smiling.

One of the first signs of Alzheimer's is a deliberate change of appearance. His mustache hangs in oiled handlebars over the ends of his mouth. It's been that way as long as I've known him, not all that long.

"Well thank yah, honey. I've been carrying it around with me for 73 years- No 63... Becky how old am I?" he asks with a crooked grin, snickering.

"You're 76, Carl." she says laughing.

"Oh, well alright."

Swinging his fist in the air, he smiles in mock victory and breaks out laughing harder than anybody else.

I guess there's something to be said for positivity, or at least senility.

A Lack of Disconnection
Ellyn Julius

Henry David Thoreau once said, "Our inventions are wont to be pretty toys, which distract our attention from serious things."(Political Writings. 59. Par. 2). Our technological advances have surpassed those of Thoreau's time and most likely anything he ever imagined. We have the capability to communicate with people anywhere in the world within seconds and post the best aspects of our lives on social media to show those people we are "friends" with on social media how great our lives are. We can search for love and intimacy online, whether it be on social media, dating websites, or in porn. Many people use these things to search for acceptance, popularity, or happiness through how many "likes" or "retweets" they receive.

 In an essay titled "The Numbing of the American Mind: Culture as Anesthetic," Thomas de Zengotita talks of how technology and media creates a fabricated reality. He states that media and the ease of spreading information via the internet and other technology are making it easy for us to pretend our lives are simpler and happier than they truly are. Zengotita explains this is because we spend so much time on social media, watching TV, and other internet sites, we get wrapped up in this idea that everything we see online and in movies is what our lives should be like. (596). The film, Disconnect, exemplifies some of the troubles of technology that Zengotita touches on, and even expands on other negative aspects.

From the surface, Disconnect may seem as if it is a

simple cautionary tale about the overuse of technology with forced and intertwined lives. However, if we look deeper into this film, it elaborately shows how technology negatively impacts relationships between family, friends and even strangers. As the movie follows the arcs of three different stories, it ultimately reveals that technology puts a non-physical distance in a relationship, distracts people from those they care about, dehumanizes people and creates a justification for the normalization of porn and the loss of intimacy.

Many people use the internet to cope with different issues in their lives. For example, there are chatrooms for people dealing with depression, grieving over the loss of a loved one or as an escape from reality. In the first story arc in Disconnect, Cindy and Derek Hull are a young couple grieving the recent loss of their infant son. Derek pulls away from his wife and distracts himself with online games; Cindy immerses herself in an online chatroom with other adults who have lost someone important to them. Cindy and Derek's relationship becomes more strained as each of them focuses more of their time on their internet distractions rather than on each other.

Cindy and Derek find out that their identities had been stolen online as a result of their internet addictions. They hire a private investigator who determines the person who stole their identities as the man that Cindy had been talking to on her grief chatroom; however, the police cannot do anything because they do not have incriminating evidence against him. Derek and Cindy decide to find evidence on their own.

As Cindy and Derek search for the man that stole their

identities, they start to cherish the little things about each other that they had lost after the death of their son. Without the distractions of their social media and online games, they worked together towards a common goal. They began to appreciate each other and rekindled their love they had thought they lost with their son.

This story arc ultimately teaches us how technology pulls people apart. Technology offers an escape from reality, but puts distance in a relationship. If and when people use the internet or other technology as coping methods such as Derek and Cindy do in their story arc; they lose the ability or want to connect with other humans face to face. If people reached out to their loved ones in times of grief and trouble instead of cowering behind a screen, they would not be as afraid of tough times, they would not be as lonely; they would eventually experience the feeling of true happiness again and have closer relationships. Cindy and Derek show this through their story arc because by the end, they embrace each other with true love. They spent time together; they experienced things together and eventually began to heal as one for the first time since the death of their son.

Not only is technology used as a coping method; it is also used for work and social media. While cell phones can be great tools that make work and communication much easier, the first major theme of the second story arc shows the potential negatives of the overuse of cell phones. The overuse of cell phones can cause people to focus on technology rather than those they care about. Rich and Lydia Boyd are a happily married couple with two teenage kids, a daughter: Abby, and a son: Ben.

Rich is a successful lawyer, but focuses on his work at all times, whether it be him checking his cell phone throughout their family dinner or spending more time at the office than with his family. Abby is a popular high school girl, and Ben is an outcast because of his love for obscure music, his shy nature, and long dark hair.

Two boys in Ben's class, Frye and Jason, impersonate a girl named Jessica Rhony online. They message Ben pretending to have similar interests, and Ben immediately connects with "her." Eventually, "Jessica" talks Ben into sending a nude picture which Frye and Jason then distribute to the entire school. Ben then goes home and reads comments posted on social media about his dirty picture. His mom comes in and asks why he is home so early because he usually has band practice. Ben tells her he is fine, and band practice was cancelled that day. As she leaves, the camera shows a tear drop down his face; showing the true pain that the distribution of his photo has caused him. The next day, Ben tries to hang himself, but his sister and her friend get him down and to the hospital. He is in a coma throughout the remainder of the movie. Once Rich discovers "Jessica," he talks to her attempting to find out if she had any reason to believe that Ben would hurt himself. Rich spends a majority of his time messaging her, or trying to find her instead of spending time at the hospital with his family. "She" reveals very little until the end, when Jason reveals to Rich that Jessica is a fake.

Once learning who "Jessica" actually was, Rich goes to Jason's house and beats up Jason's father Mike, accidentally injuring Jason in the process. Mike immediately runs to his son to ensure he is okay. This leads to Rich speeding to the hospital where he runs to Ben's room and embraces his wife and daughter and grabs the hand of his unconscious son. He replies to his wife's worried questions of whether he was okay with "I am now." The near loss of his son caused him to rethink his priorities and realize that his family is more important that work, and he had no need to be plugged into his phone at all times.

Henry David Thoreau talks of a lesson that Rich learn by the end of the film. This lesson was about truly living your life for the important things. Thoreau does this by going to live in the wilderness. He explains his reasoning in his essay, "From Where I Lived, And What I Lived For," explaining that he went to live away from civilization so he could focus on the crucial parts of live. He describes that he wanted to make sure to engage himself in the true meaning of life so that when it came time for him to die, he did not look back on his life with regret that he simply existed rather than taking advantage of the opportunity to truly live his life. (573)

By the end of the film, Rich grasps the importance of his family and the unimportance of work in comparison. He realizes that life is fragile, and we are only here for a short amount of time; during that time, we need to make the most with the ones that matter most. We should not waste our lives plugged into our cell phones constantly worrying about work.

While the path with the Boyd family teaches us of the negatives of the overuse of cell phones, it also expresses how social media dehumanizes us. Disconnect shows this with Jason and Frye and how they treat Ben. When they are first talking to Ben as

Jessica, they think it is funny; they think that messing with him is a good way to pass time. When Ben tries to kill himself, it is a reality check for Frye, but especially Jason. When Jason talked to Ben as "Jessica" when Frye wasn't around, he connected with Ben. Jason told him that his mom died, and tells him how he feels like he is living in jail with his dad. In a scene where Jason and Frye are messaging Ben, things start to become deep and personal. Jason feels bad for creating this fake person that Ben is connecting with and then sending the picture around. When Frye sees Jason's remorse, he laughs and then says, "Do you feel sorry for him?" and "Are you in love with him?" Jason snaps out of it and laughs it off, playfully punching Frye and exclaiming how gross and dumb he was being. Until Ben tried to kill himself, they did not truly realize what they were saying and what they did hurt Ben as much as it did.

Social media makes it easy for people to harass and bully other people because they do not seem real online. You cannot see the person; you cannot see that your words and actions hurt them and you cannot see how that person reacts. All of communication performed over social media is a simple form of communication. We are unable to hear how a person responds to our comments so it makes it effortless to harass someone online. Jason and Frye did not realize the effect of their words and actions until Ben tried to kill himself, and when Jason visited him in the hospital, it humanized Ben. Jason realized that Ben was not just something to mess with online; he was a real human being with feelings.

Social media and the internet can dehumanize people

in different ways. One way is the ease of harassing others; another is the sexualization and dehumanization through porn and adult only chatrooms/ video chatrooms. The final story arc attacks this problem with a reporter, Nina Dunham, who meets a teen performer on an adult entertainment site named Kyle. Kyle is a member of a house of teenaged kids who perform on this adult entertainment site. Nina finds his story interesting so she connects with him on the site. She flirts with him and eventually pays him to talk face to face on video chat. Nina deceives him and convinces him to meet her in person by implying that she will have sex with him. When they meet, she tells him that she wants to feature him in a story and promises she will not reveal his identity. The story airs, and the police want Nina to tell them where the house is with all of the teens from the website. She does not know but once it is discovered that she paid Kyle to connect with him, she is reprimanded because it was potentially illegal and completely unethical. She is suspended from work and uses that time to try and figure out where the house is. She convinces Kyle to give her the address, which she hands over to the police. The house leader is tipped off and evacuates the house before the police raid it. Nina attempts to find Kyle and once she does, she takes off to rescue him instead of informing the police. The house leader beats Nina on she arrives at the hotel and then leaves with all of the teens, including Kyle, leaving Nina injured on the parking lot.

Kyle told Nina that he did not want her to rescue him; he enjoyed what he did; and he felt empowered by it. That statement in itself is a problem. The normalization of porn has made it seem okay to reveal yourself to strangers, to pleasure yourself in front of them. Special, intimate, and private acts have now become available at our fingertips making them less special as to when they are performed with someone you love.

Omar M. Bradley, a late five star general who fought in North Africa and Europe during WWII, talked of if we continue to grow our technology without some sort caution and good-judgement, then we may become killers of ourselves. (no page). Disconnect represents this thought with great aplomb. It shows that when we turn to the internet to find solace in a time of hurt, we will not find what we are looking for; if we direct all of our attention to our cell phones, we will miss out on experiences with our loved ones. It shows that social media has created this false idea that the people on the other end of harassing messages are not real people. It shows how pornography has sexualized people and how it creates a lack of intimacy between real lovers.

We should seek solace in the arms of a loved one. We should direct our attention to the ones in our lives that matter, because they could be gone without warning. We should realize that everyone we talk to on social media is a human being capable of feeling pain and rethink that rude message that we were about to send. Finally, we should eliminate porn and the false sense of intimacy it creates.

If we refuse to change, we will become slaves of technology; humans incapable of having interaction with one another unless it is over a text, webcam, internet chat, e-mail, or social media. We will no longer be humans capable of feeling intimacy, love and true happiness. We will become robots, methodically going about our days, only to die alone with the regret that we only simply existed.

Sources

Bradley, Omar. Armistice Day Address. Boston, Massachusetts. 11 Nov. 1948. Speech.

de Zengotita, Thomas. "The Numbing of the American Mind: Culture as Anesthetic." Reading Popular Culture. Ed. Michael Keller. Dubuque, IA. Kendall Hunt, 2015. 595-605. Print.

Thoreau, Henry David. Thoreau: Political Writings-Selections from Walden. Ed. Nancy L.   Rosenblum. Cambridge, UK: Cambridge University Press, 1996. Print.

Thoreau, Henry David. "From Where I Lived, And What I Lived For." Reading Popular Culture. Ed. Michael Keller. Dubuque, IA. Kendall Hunt, 2015. 573-579. Print.

Sanctuary
Angela Blake

The bells tolled.
Shapes of small voices
coming through as hymnals
that shared sweet sounds across
all the rooms we rested. Tugs on toes
from the foot of the bed begged for action
in the kitchen. Plinks of O's on old plum bowls.
Then retreat to the church of sheets with new prayers
of lace and flickering lights through the flats of window
pews
to warmed honey walls.

Sorghum
Angela Blake

The cheap and disgraceful mark of painted blue trailer
rubs off onto too short, stone washed jeans. A no
money smell
fills the air from the sorghum
factory down the way by the dry river,
bed cracked in anger from a sun
bent on burning life to the core.

A home where girls named DeeDee and Sherry
brought bugs into beds where they kissed
and touched things wrong.
A steady stream of train runs south
of the gravel mounds, a mothers fear.
Where children hide themselves in caves
while dust laughingly swims into their lungs.

The chow mutts howl and hell,
from wagons too close to their cage and chains.
And children are summoned from cement
steps to collect their bologna and cheese
on white.

on the matter of death
Angela Blake

it's a brick burying into your clavicles
it's a wandering ghost running in your cells
it's a sadness that seeps into the holes of your bones
it's a stagger in your lungs when you try to exhale
it's a pain that fractures your sound into bits when you
scream
it's a bottle in your lap with no more drink to dry you
up

it's a shudder up your spine that ends in your fingertips
it's a burning in your hands that hisses with a knuckle
bend
it's a pull in your center that won't let go until you're
inside out

it's a hum in your jaw that rakes into your ears
it's a push of a sob so far down that it collapses into a
pit
it's a burn deep in your lips from the pull of cigarette
paper
it's a racing in your eyes that won't rest
it's a rumble of stones boiling in your belly
it's a gnawing in your teeth from uncontrollable
pressure
it's a curl in your shoulders like a wood shaving in
winter

it's a shake in your middle that moves the house in jolts

252

My Father's Sons
Rachel Howard

"I'm sorry," was the phrase I remembered uttering most in my father's presence as a child. "I'm sorry," I said, as I eyed the arrow that had clattered pathetically at my feet. His brown eyes were steady as he regarded me from his monumental height. He had taken my brother and me out into the field that day for our first target practice. My father had decided to leave no stone unturned when it came to raising us. With our mother passed on before we could remember, I guess he was afraid he would forget something. Almost every week, he seemed to come up with a new skill we needed to learn—fishing, splitting wood, hoeing, and the like. And now it was high time we started learning how to hunt. We had guns, of course—two old rifles that my father kept on the top shelf in the kitchen—but he insisted that we learn bow hunting first. He had set up a small target made of rough wood, two white circles etched onto it in chalk.

My twin brother, Oliver, went first. He and I shared the same red-brown hair, freckles, and our mother's green eyes. Our father always told us we were lucky to have our mother's beautiful eyes. Oliver and I would have looked exactly alike, except that it looked as though someone had sucked all of the strength out of my body and put it into his. He had the healthy, robust look of a child who spent his time running outdoors, while my delicate physique suggested illness or poverty. It was true I spent more time poring over the few books in our tiny cabin than sprinting through the fields, but it was more that I just could not seem to grow. The tiny bow and arrow our father had fashioned had seemed to fit naturally into Oliver's strong, assured hands. He pulled it back and let fly—the arrow had happily stuck just left of the center of the target.

My father crossed to pluck the arrow from the target. The corners of his eyes crinkled as he smiled, unable to hide his pride.

"Not bad, Oliver." He nodded toward my brother. "Your turn, Erik."

I took the arrow from my father and the bow from my brother, carefully arranging them in my hands the way we had been taught. They felt awkward and stiff in my hands; my fingers were clumsy as I nocked the arrow. I pulled back, trying to copy the way Oliver had done it. The string slipped out of my grasp.

My father sighed. "It's all right, son." I watched his face, and did not miss the way his smile had decayed, though he tried to hide it. "Just... more practice." He turned to Oliver. "Help him, won't you? You two can stay out here with the target for a while."

"Yes, sir," Oliver replied, stooping to pick up the arrow.

I felt a lump in my throat as I watched my father walk

back to the house.

***

I stepped into the quiet kitchen, clutching a suitcase in each hand. Everything I owned was packed neatly into them. The pale morning sunlight shone through the one small window as I met my father's eyes.

"Today's the day," he said, glancing at the bags.

"Yes, sir," I replied, mustering a smile. I set the bags down on the wooden table. I couldn't help but notice that my acceptance letter to the University of Virginia still sat gathering dust on one corner of the table. I had won a scholarship, too—otherwise, my father would never have been able to afford to send me.

Oliver stepped into the kitchen from the sitting room adjoining.

"Well, I guess our scholar's leaving us," he said. Grinning, he pulled me into a bear hug that lifted me off the ground and pinned my arms to my sides. Growing up had been good to him—he was tall and strong, and about twice my size. He set me down and clapped a hand on my shoulder. "I'll miss you, brother."

"Don't worry—I'll write. Every week," I assured him.

"Don't let them make you into a fancy gentleman at that school," Oliver teased, eyes twinkling.

"Right, Dad?"

"I'm sure Erik'll be fine," my father replied. He glanced out the window. "Oliver—don't you think you ought to be going? Don't want to be late."

"Oh, right!" Oliver grabbed his cap from the hook by the door and slapped it onto his head. He had already been working in the mine for about two weeks now, like our father—who was finally retiring, now that Oliver was taking over—and his father before him.

"Safe travels, Erik!" Oliver called over his shoulder. "Don't forget to come home once in a while!"

"Be careful, son!" my father called after Oliver as he bounded out the door.

"I will!" we heard him call from outside. I watched my father watch my brother disappear into the distance out the window.

After a moment, my father looked at me. "Well, hadn't you better be going too?"

"Yes," I said, gathering my suitcases, "Yes, sir."

***

My entire body shook as I raised my fist to knock on the door of the old farmhouse; it had nothing to do with the rain that plastered my hair to my face. My other hand clutched only one suitcase, containing only a few things packed hurriedly amid the frenzy. I should

256

have come home before now; maybe that would have made this easier. I hadn't even been writing anymore— I had managed one letter the semester before. Swallowing hard, I knocked. I stood frozen, hoping in spite of myself that no one would come to the door.

I jumped as the door swung open.

"Dad, I—" I stopped as I caught sight of Oliver's green eyes.

"Erik." He looked at me. It had only been two years, but he looked older. Hard labor had worn away at his jovial features. He was somber now, looking at me as if I was a stranger he was trying to remember where he'd seen before. "Well, come in then," he said, attempting a smile.

The house had hardly changed at all, the kitchen as sparse and tidy as ever. I shivered as the heat of the small stove overtook my rain-soaked body. My brother and I stood on opposite ends of the table, looking at one another.

"Dad...?"

"He's upstairs," Oliver said, "He'll have heard you come in. He should be down soon."

"Oliver, the letter—"

My brother looked down. "I didn't see it. Dad told me."

"Erik." My father had appeared at the kitchen door, brows knit as he studied me.

"Dad," I choked, unable to look him in the face. "I'm... I'm sorry. I'm so sorry."

"Is it true, Erik?"

I looked up, and noticed the parchment clutched in my father's fist. I could just make out the university's insignia in the top-right corner. It was the letter that had ruined me—the letter the university wrote after a professor caught me with Tobias Hanger in the library after hours, locked in an embrace that was more than friendly. I knew Toby's family had received the same one.

"Is it true?" my father repeated.

I hung my head. Tears welled up in my eyes. "Yes, sir."

Silence reigned for what seemed like hours. Finally, I couldn't take it. "I'm sorry, Dad," I blurted, "I never meant... I'm sorry."

"There's going to be a trial?"

"Yes."

"Are you going to lose?"

"I... I don't know, sir."

He was silent again for a while, studying his worn

leather boots. Finally, he spoke. "Is it what you want, Erik?"

"Dad," interjected Oliver, "Don't you think—"

"Let him answer," said my father.

"I'm... I don't know," I whispered.

My father crossed the room until he stood directly in front of me. He put a hand on my shoulder. His face was grave. "You don't belong here, son. Go back to the city." He took a deep breath, regarding me evenly. "And good luck."

***

They never recovered the body, the letter had said. There was to be a funeral, but no casket. He was one of many who had been lost in the mine's collapse. I had not seen him in ten years... I had stayed away, assumed they did not want to see me.

I met my father standing in front of the old house. He did not look like the man I remembered. His proud shoulders were stooped; the warmth had gone out of his laugh-crinkled eyes. He tried to smile when he saw me.

"Son," he said, choking on the word, "You've... changed. You look well."

"Thanks." I had changed. The charges against me had been dropped—Toby's family had paid a famous lawyer to tell the story. Toby's grandmother had just passed on, and I was only comforting him. Only one professor had seen us, after all. It was dark; surely he couldn't tell if we hadn't simply clasped one another in manly camaraderie. Inconclusive evidence. We were allowed to continue school, but he transferred to a college in New York. We never spoke again.

After graduation, I had been awarded a position on a research team, and spent several years traveling in South America. The years had treated me well—travel and more time in the sun had banished my sickly pallor and added a bit more substance to my thin figure. Sometimes, when I caught sight of my reflection in a window, I'd think I'd seen my brother.

"Dad... I... I'm sorry."

My father did not even try to hide the tears in his eyes. "You got my letter?"

"Yes, sir."

"Didn't know how to find you... had to write to your old school." He sniffled. "The mine collapsed... your brother—"

"I know, Dad. I know."

Abruptly, my father threw his arms around my

shoulders. "My son," he whispered, "I'm sorry, Erik."

And my father wept onto my chest. After a moment, he released me, wiping his eyes with a calloused hand. "I should've written you before... we were so glad to hear you'd gotten back into the school."

"I wish I had been here... I should've taken the time... I'm sorry, Dad."

My father's eyes crinkled into his familiar smile. "Well, son," he said, "I should have too."

The Bard
Rachel Howard

My wrists and ankles were bound to the wall with tight shackles. The lashes across my back throbbed with pain as they pressed into the rough stone. I smelled terrible... a rancid piece of meat on a butcher's hook. My arms ached as if they would explode from being held upward for so long... I did not know how long I had been here. The room was not large—the walls and floor were the same damp, gray stone. The only furnishing was a wooden table that held the man's tools—his knives, his chains, whips, and others I didn't know the names of. There was only one door and no windows; a single sputtering torch cast a noxious glow about the chamber. Now came the pain... my only respite from the dark, lonely hours strapped to the wall. I whimpered as the man brandished the wide, red-hot iron close to my face.

"Last chance, pretty boy," said the oily voice. The man always wore a hood that covered all but his eyes— gray eyes, strangely light, open too wide and filled with bloodlust. It was always the same man—I knew him. I knew his eyes and his voice and the careful manner in which he handled his tools. "You don't confess right here, right now, you won't be so pretty by the time I'm done with you." The eyes glinted.

"I don't know what you're talking about!" I

squeaked, trying to arch my body away from the hot iron. I didn't want it... not on my face. I'd always been handsome—I remembered ladies in bright-colored dresses telling me so. They loved my eyes—emerald, they said—and my hair. My hair was ruined—I could see it hanging in front of my face; it was matted, filthy... the chestnut turned to dull gray-brown. But I still had my face.

"Please..." I begged.

"That's it? You refuse?"

"I don't know anything... I've told you! Please... I'm just a bard..." I insisted. Just a bard. As the heat of the iron moved closer, beads of sweat began to form on my forehead.

"You'll regret that." I could hear the cruel smile in the man's voice.

"Please! No no no no—"

And the iron was on my face, burning me, singing my skin. I screamed. The agony sent angry waves through my brain, making me see red behind my eyes. The smell of smoke and burned flesh poured from under the iron.

Over the sound of my own incoherent screaming, I was vaguely aware of the voice.

"Confess, scum! Or the gods help me—"

I couldn't speak. The iron pressed harder into my face, burning deeper. I felt it hit bone. I screamed again, unable to form words.

"You asked for it, you little worm." He sounded giddy. The iron was removed from my face. The area surged with hot pain, and I couldn't see out of my left eye. I felt my breeches jerked down. I heaved and sobbed—he did not always do this. But sometimes the man would have a bad day—he would need the entire canvas of my body for his grisly art. There were already scars forming everywhere from my shoulders to my ankles. My torturer was thorough, intimate. I was dimly aware of the man's blurry figure taking a long, curved knife from the table. I started to... laugh. It did not sound like me at all. I could not stop it. It was not human. My voice rose beyond my control, cackling and yelping frantically through my pain and my tears like some freakish livestock animal driven mad in a slaughterhouse.

The man had left me lying in a pool of my own blood, the door slightly ajar. He thought I was dead. I was horrified that I was not. I had clawed my way across the room to the door, desperately trying to keep my eyes from wandering to the thing lying in the blood next to me. I had to get away... I could not stand it. I would die, but I would not die here, lying in blood, surrounded by stone walls... no. No.

264

Something inside me set afire. I seized my breeches and struggled into them—I did not want to look at myself. I kept crawling... it was dark, no one was there, no one stopped me... my hands hit something dry and rough among the stone—it was wood. I found a metal handle in the center—a trap door. I seized the handle and threw myself to one side, managing to swing the door open in a feverish burst of strength. The sound of gurgling water reached my ears. Below, a dim, gray glow illuminated a shallow stream of dark water several feet under the trap door. I threw myself in, breaking the fall with my hands as I landed in the ankle-deep stream. The water was frigid and foul smelling—a sewer of sorts, and I continued to crawl though it.

Finally, I reached a small pool of pale light. Wooden bars had rotted away from a tiny opening. I squeezed through it, and found myself blinking in the blinding light of outdoors. It was cold—late winter, I guessed. I squinted as my eyes adjusted, and realized that I was outside the fortress's grim walls. I scrambled to the bank of the tiny pool, and forced myself to my feet. I could feel my adrenaline running out, but I would not be taken back into the dungeon. I could not stand properly—my weak back kept me doubled over, but I saw the forest's edge not a league away. Willing forth the last scraps of strength within me, I ran. I ran until I could run no more.

My legs gave out, knees buckling underneath me. I landed hard on my knees, near-bare bones crashing

against the frozen earth. I had made it into a wood—
bare, skeletal trees rose around the small clearing
where I had fallen. A wave of pain from my groin
overwhelmed me. I moaned, eyes moving involuntarily
down. A fresh pool of dark red was spreading on my
already filthy, bloodstained breeches. My stomach
roiled, and I fell forward to my hands. I could not
remember the last time I had eaten, and still my
stomach heaved, trying to vomit. I could feel my ribs
against my skin, projecting as if they would break
through. Gagging and coughing, I lowered my face to
the ground, supporting my forehead with a hand so
that the burns on my face would not touch the frost. A
foul smell reached me--a rancid stink of excrement and
blood and rot. My stomach heaved again—I lifted my
head to avoid the stench. I could feel the hot blood
running down my thighs. I could not—would not—
look. It made no difference. I was going to die.

I turned over to lie on my back. The lashes across
it burned in protest, but subsided as the cold numbed
them. I lay with my legs splayed apart, trying not to feel
the wet emptiness between them. Another influx of
agony surged from the area, and I cried out aloud.
Tears filled my eyes, quickly brimming and falling down
the sides of my face. They burned as they slid across
the charred flesh.

Why? I thought. Oh, gods, why? I'm just a bard...
was just a bard.

I hadn't asked to be caught in the crossfire of the attack on Lord Tharn's keep. I had only been trying to make a few pounds playing my fiddle at the court. I could remember the big windows in the hall, my music spinning up into the high ceiling... and then the horns outside... wailing. I couldn't help that I had been the same age as the lord's heir, or that young Vander had managed to escape before Reynwood's forces had broken through. Vander and I could have been brothers. They had taken me... did not believe I was who I said. I had done nothing to deserve this—it had nothing to do with me. Even when the jailors had realized that I wasn't Vander—and I knew they had— they didn't make the man stop. Always the same man... I knew him, a sick man... I wondered what he would do when he saw that I was gone...

I did not know how long I lay there. I was vaguely conscious of the cold, of the pain... but it was slipping. My vision was fading, my mind traveling further and further from me, and I knew I was dying. My slowing breaths rattled in my lungs.

I was not afraid of death. I had known death was coming for me from the day I had awakened in the dungeon. And so I lay on the frozen earth of the forest, waiting for death to wrap me in its embrace.

"Can you hear me, my son?"

My consciousness came rushing back, and with it

267

the pain. Its sudden return made me gasp. I opened my eyes. A figure hovered over me, crouching beside me. A large man, I thought, though my unfocused eyes could not make out his face. My mind told me that I should get away, but my limbs refused to respond.

"I am a healer," the stranger said slowly, softly brushing my singed, matted hair away from my face. His voice was quiet and sonorous—a safe sound. It had been months since I had heard a kind voice. I tried to speak, but my voice cracked.

"Do not be afraid, my son," said the healer. "I heal all creatures who have need in this forest. I will do for you what I can. Will you come with me?"

I realized that I had not spoken since I had been tortured for the last time. I tried again, but only managed a rasping moan.

"Hush," he said whispered, gently supporting my head with a large hand. "Drink this. It will bring sleep." There was a flask at my lips. The liquid made me gag and burned my throat, but filled me immediately with warmth. I felt myself being lifted from the ground and wrapped in a cloak. Strong arms raised my emaciated form and carried me a short distance. I heard the snorting and pawing of a horse. I closed my eyes.

I woke up in a bed. It was soft and warm; I had blankets and a pillow. I was vaguely conscious of firelight. I thought this must be a dream, or perhaps I was dead. A slight shifting of my legs told me I was not. I grimaced at the recollection, and waiting for the onslaught of pain. It didn't come. I sat up, blinking in the dim light. I was in a small, tidy wood-walled room. A well-tended fire crackled happily in the hearth, and rough-spun curtains covered the little window.

I pulled back the covers. I was naked except for bandages, but I had needed so many that they covered me well enough. With a start, I realized that I was clean. I had been so long covered in grime that I had nearly forgotten what color my skin was. Bandages wrapped around my chest and back, as well as my wrists and ankles. A particularly thick wrapping wound around my waist and between my legs. I winced at the flatness there. I brought my hands to my face, and found a bandage wrapped from my left cheekbone angling up to my forehead, leaving space for my eyes. A wave of panic washed over me. My face... I remembered. I touched my hair. A small, involuntary smile played across my lips as a lock of thick, wavy chestnut tumbled in front of my eyes.

I turned to sit on the side of the bed, carefully lowering my bare feet to the floor. My knees buckled— I quickly clutched bedpost to keep myself from falling. Unsteady, and holding fast to the bedpost, I stood straight. Something next to me clattered to the floor—

a carved cane. I leaned over to pick it up, and arranged it in my hand. I looked across the room. On a wooden chair next to the closed door laid a neatly folded stack of clothes. Planting my feet, I let go of the bedpost. I leaned heavily on the cane, but my legs held. My stride was shaky as I approached the chair. My legs were stiff, my body felt strange and light. I reached the chair and supported myself on it, leaning the cane against the wall. The clothes, a cloth tunic and breeches, and woolen stockings, would have been far too large for me even before. Now, I had lost so much body mass that they drowned me, but I shrugged into them anyway, winding the woven belt tightly around my shrunken waist to make them stay. It felt good to wear soft, clean clothes. I hugged my arms around myself, savoring the warmth. I remembered the man in the woods. He should not have taken the trouble... heart in my throat, I took the cane in hand and opened the door.

The cabin's main room was large and high ceilinged, and as warm and tidy as the smaller bedroom. A massive fire burned in an elaborately carved shoulder-high fireplace. In a high-backed chair next to the hearth sat the largest man I had ever seen. Upon hearing my entrance, the giant turned to face me. He was not truly a giant, but he must have been at least seven feet tall if he had been standing, and his entire body seemed to be made of bulging, stone-hard muscle. He was dressed in a tunic and breeches similar to the ones he had left for me, with a fur cloak draped over his shoulders and enormous leather boots. Despite his monumental size, the most striking thing about him was his face. I could not put an age to the face; it was a face weathered by the elements and full of wisdom, but filled with all the joy and handsomeness of youth. The man's thick, dark beard matched his long hair. His eyes, pools of deepest green, crinkled at the corners, were merry and kind. He smiled at me as I entered the room.

"They are rather too large for you, child," he apologized, "But I hope they will keep you warm."

"Yes," I said, my voice weak and hoarse. I cleared my throat. "Thank you. For everything you've done." I dropped my eyes. "But you should have let me die."

I brought my eyes back to look at the giant, whose face now wore expression of deep sadness. "How could I leave you to die, my son? I am a healer; I heal all those who have need. I leave no creature broken that can yet be mended."

My face burned with shame. "But... I can't be..." I said, my voice barely above a whisper, "You know... you saw..."

The great man bowed his head. "Sit down, my son," he said, gesturing to the other chair at the fire.

Leaning on the cane like a man three times my

age, I approached the hearth. I gingerly arranged myself in the huge chair. My limbs did not seem move properly; I felt awkward and gangly.

"What is your name, child?" asked the healer.

"Orriyin Strain."

"Orriyin Strain. My name is Borun. I am the guardian of this forest and of all goodly creatures in it, both sentient and beast. It is my duty and my privilege to tend to those who need my art. It is mine to see that no living being dies before its time within the borders of my land." The giant's voice rumbled as he spoke. "Now, my son," he continued, "Why do you think you should have died?"

"Because--" My voice broke as humiliated tears filled my eyes. "I'm broken."

"Do not cry, child," chided Borun, "You will ruin your bandages." I dried my eyes and tried to stop. "I am truly and deeply sorry for what has been done to you, Orriyin Strain," continued Borun, "But I say you are not broken."

"But I am." I was no longer a man; I was unnatural, a freak.

Borun's forehead creased as he seemed to read my thoughts. He sighed, remaining silent for a moment. "What is it that you do, Orriyin Strain?" he asked at length.

"I'm just a bard," I replied.

"A bard is a very important person. A bard brings joy to the lands to which he travels."

"Or, I was a bard."

"Are you no longer?"

I was silent. I had not thought about my future... I had never imagined that I would live.

"What did you do when you were a bard?"

"Well, I..." I cleared my throat again. My voice was returning. "I mostly traveled to different cities and villages. Playing and singing in taverns. Sometimes courts."

"When you have healed, my son, there is no reason you cannot again do these things."

"But I... I haven't..."

"It is not what you haven't, my son," said Borun, "But what you have. Have you not feet?"

"Yes--"

"Then travel. Have you not hands?"

"Yes--"

"Then play. Have you not your voice?"

"I think so—"

"Then sing, my son," said Borun, taking my thin hands in his huge ones. "You are more than a body. No one can break your spirit unless you allow them to do so." He squeezed my hands. "I say you are not broken, but whole." His voice grew in volume and conviction. "And I say you shall not die, but live."

A warm, tingling sensation flowed from Borun's hands into mine. The feeling surged through my arms and into my shoulders, then flowed down to culminate in my chest. It rested there like excitement, like joy. My face broke in a true smile.

"I suppose I'll have to find new instruments," I mused after a moment. I'd lost both my fiddle and mandolin.

Borun smiled knowingly and rose from his chair, towering over me. He crossed the room to a tall bookshelf and pulled a cloth-wrapped object from the top. He brought it back to the hearth and sat again, handing the parcel to me.

I pulled back the cloth and removed a beautiful harp of polished wood. It was carved with birds and leaves, which seemed almost to flit and rustle as the dark wood gleamed in the firelight. Holding it, a smaller version of the joyful sensation tingled in my hands. I gave the strings a light strum, my fingertips delighting in the motion. The music that emanated from the harp sounded somehow like sunlight and like clear running water, like the tinkling of icicles and like birdsong. I stared and the beautiful instrument for a moment before remembering myself. I met Borun's eyes, which were crinkling in the brightest of smiles.

"How did you know...?" I gasped.

"Your spirit is strong," the healer said. "My art extends beyond the healing of the body. Even in your black sleep, music rang strong within your soul. My herbs and bandages will heal your body; this harp is my remedy to heal your mind."

"Thank you," I breathed, "Thank you." I could not think of words enough.

"I know you will use it well, my son," replied Borun.

The tears in my eyes were joyous tears this time, and I knew that I would survive.

The Lord of the Longships
Rachel Howard

"The Lord of the Longships appeared unlooked for that day. The mainlanders were ravaging our city—defeat seemed certain. Until he came, that is. A thick fog was his harbinger; voices whispered through the mist as he approached, voices that sang a distant and ancient song, voices that were not entirely human. His boats were empty, but the oars were down, rowing as though manned by a thousand strong sailors." The old man paused to puff on his pipe, relishing the tale. It was one he never tired of telling. The raging storm outside the little fishing cottage and the firelight's dancing on the weathered walls made the perfect background too. The grandfather smiled. "His tattered banner bore a single red slash so vivid it tore through the fog. And the Lord himself stood alone at the helm of his flagship. He was a slight figure clad in ragged robes of deep green, bareheaded but for a circlet of splintered wood. As his fleet drew near, he reached out his hands. Three fingers remained on his right hand; on his left, two. His face was hollow and grim, his eyes empty."

"What happened to his fingers, Grandfather?" the younger boy asked, enraptured. The last time the old man had been to visit, the boy had been too young to remember stories.

"No one knows, you sod," the older brother snapped. He had heard the tale of the Lord of the Longships at least twice.

276

The old man patiently drew in on his pipe, and then blew a wide smoke ring. The younger boy, and the older in spite of himself, gigged in awe at the trick. "Now," the old man said, "Are you two going to let me get on with my story?"

"Yes, Grandfather!" the younger boy cried. He absentmindedly rubbed at the bruise recently inflicted upon his forehead by his older brother in a now-forgotten tussle.

"Hmm..." the old man stroked his beard, feigning forgetfulness. "Where was I?"

"His eyes were empty!" the elder brother prompted.

"Ah, yes," the old man said, settling deeper into the rocking chair. A roll of thunder rattled the cottage, making the boys' eyes twinkle with fearful glee. "His eyes were empty, but he could see our need. The war was terrible, you see—I was only about your age, but I remember. Entire cities destroyed. Warships sunk. Thousands dead. I had been out collecting clams with my mother that day, when we suddenly saw ships on the horizon. The alarm was sounded, and our soldiers ran down to the beach to meet them. My mother pulled me underneath a dock with her. We prayed that we would be spared. The mainlanders fell upon us; there were thousands of them. Our men fought with true islander courage, but there were just too many of them. I was terrified—"

"Until the Lord of the Longships came!" blurted the older boy.

"Yes indeed," the old man chuckled. "I knew him as soon as his grey ships on the horizon. The legends told us that the Lord of the Longships brought death to tyrants wherever he appeared." He leaned forward, lowering his voice. "And just like in the legends, he raised his hands to command the waters, and the vast mainland army was rent asunder. Ravenous waves swept up the beach, pulling the mainlanders down into the Lord's domain. With my own eyes, I saw dozens of men dragged into the sea by the waters, but not a single islander was among them."

"What happened then, Grandfather?" asked the smaller boy.

 "Well," the grandfather continued, leaning back in his chair, "We rescued souls knelt before him on the beach. We cried for him to come ashore, hailing him as our king."

"But he didn't come, did he, Grandfather?" recalled the elder boy.

"No he did not," the old man replied. "That is not his way. No, the Lord's clear, distant eyes never fell upon us. Our cheers and homage never reached his ears. Instead he looked down upon the green sea, bent his fair head, and raised his arms. Grey fog enfolded the ghostly fleet, and when it cleared, the Lord of the

Longships had vanished."

"Did you ever see him again, Grandfather?" The smaller boy's eyes were wide with wonder.

"Our course not," his older brother replied. "You heard Grandfather. That isn't his way."

"But who is he?" the younger asked. "What is he?"

The grandfather inhaled deeply again on his pipe. He glanced out the window in the direction of the raging grey sea. "Some say that the Lord of the Longships was the son of a sea-god, angered by the slaughter that men's armies committed upon his domain. The god sent his own flesh and blood, imbued with the powers of the mighty waves and crushing depths, to smite the evil men that had come to prowl the seas. The Lord, it was said, would not return to his kingdom below until the waves had been cleansed of the blood of innocents."

"Others claim that the Lord of the Longships was the ghost of a seafaring king of olden times, a great warrior whose homeland was taken by marauders. The great Lord, unable to rest, was doomed to sail until the end of time, searching for peoples in danger of sharing his fate. Until the end of days will the Lord sail in exile, protecting the freedom of those who could not protect themselves."

"What do you think, Grandfather?" the older boy

asked. He had never heard this part of the story.

The old man thoughtfully stroked his long, grey beard. "A humble few of us," he began, "Say that the Lord of Longships was once an arrogant young islander prince who betrayed his brother in search of glory. You see, there was another great war between the mainland and the islands long before my time. The foolish prince was defeated in battle, captured by his brother's men, and flung into the sea. Just before he drowned, a mighty sea-spirit took pity upon the broken prince and granted him a means of redemption. She raised him up as her champion, bestowing upon him the arts of sea-changing. In return, he is charged to protect her waves from those who would harm peaceful sea-peoples and fated to never again set foot upon any shore." He paused, allowing the story to sink in. "That is what I think."

His two grandsons looked up at him in awe.

"He killed his brother?" the older boy asked.

"So the legend goes."

The boy glanced at the bruise on his brother's forehead. "Was he the older brother?"

"Now, that I cannot say," the grandfather replied. "But regardless, he teaches us that we must remain loyal to our families."

"But the spirit turned the prince into a powerful Lord," the younger brother said.
"That's not so bad."

"True, he received power," the grandfather admitted. He rose from his chair and crossed to the fireplace, knocking the ashes from his pipe into the hearth. "But his power came at a great price. Think of it—he must sail the seas forever, never setting foot on land or coming to a place he can call his home."

"Never?" the older brother asked.

The grandfather looked at the boys, and noticed that the elder had placed his arm around the younger's shoulder's. He smiled. "Never. He is cursed to sail the seas until the end of time."

***

The rope around Sephyr's neck was just short enough to keep his head bent to the ground, forcing him to stare at the boulder the other end was attached to. His hands and feet were bloody, unrecognizable appendages. He grimaced in pain as tears rolled down his cheeks. He had only wanted to be important for once... to do something meaningful...

"Sephyr, son of King Faren, former Prince of the Island Kingdom," the general recited. "You have been charged with kinslaying, the murder of your brother, the Prince Ero, and the betrayal of your countrymen to our enemies. You have been found guilty, and are

sentenced to death by drowning. May the gods have
mercy on you."

Two strong men picked up the stone before him.

"No, wait! Please, I'll do anythi—"

It was too late. The colossal weight of the boulder
propelled him forward and down beneath the surface,
into the murky grey-green tomb that was the sea.
Unthinking in his panic, he tried to scream, but only
bubbles were expelled from his open mouth. He
thrashed in panic as his lungs filled with water. The
unrelenting boulder pulled him ever downward.

The boulder hit something solid—the sea's floor. The
sun was now a pale distant circle dancing on the wavy
ceiling high above. He could feel the pressure closing in
and knew it would be over soon, but still he flailed his
useless limbs.

Suddenly, out of the gloom, a ghostly figure emerged.
His eyes widened. As the shape moved toward him, it
took on the form of a woman, young and slender, clad
in a robe of seaweed. She walked on the floor of the
ocean as if it were dry land, her steps swift and
assured. She was close enough now that he could see
her face—luminous against the shadowy darkness,
beautiful and wild, smiling at him. The pressure in his
lungs threatened to explode his body as he made a
desperate attempt to reach for her. Her smile widened,
and she nodded. Then, his world was black.

***

The rumble of a passing wave made the young man start out of bed with a shout, eyes wide with terror, his voice echoing through the cavernous chamber. She braced her hands against his shoulders, hushing him. She was glad she had stayed with him this night. His fear was no help to her.

"It is only the sea," she whispered, coaxing him back into a lying position. "The sea is home, child." Poor creature. She had found him not three weeks ago, defeated and pathetic. A kinslayer, they'd said—a murderer—a well-deserved casualty from the spat between the island kingdom and the mainland. She probably would have accepted him as a sacrifice immediately if she had not felt the glint of power within him.

"Sleep now," she said softly, taking one of his broken hands in hers. Three fingers remained on the hand-- his small finger, forefinger, and thumb. On the other were only two, the forefinger and the middle. He was missing toes too; he did not walk well. But he could learn again.

"I'm afraid to sleep," the young man whimpered. "What if Ero—"

"No." She firmly squeezed his hand. "He is dead. He is no more. If there were ghosts here, I could see them."

283

He only stared up at her, his eyes clouded, whimpering.

"No ghosts come here," she told him, taking his other hand. She willed a small stream of strength through her veins into his. She could not begin his training until he was stronger. "Do you believe me?"

"Yes... yes," he finally replied, his eyes looking more focused.

"Then sleep, weary one. You must rest. Your strength will return to you soon."

"Yes..." His eyelids lowered, her magic working on him. She reached out and stroked his hair, then leaned down and kissed his forehead. "Rest well," she murmured.

His eyes dropped closed as her kiss flowed through him. He was, in a way, beautiful, she thought as his breathing became deep and slow. He had been handsome, she could tell, before the war. Now, his face was sunken and hollow, lined from terror and duress-- but his now was a fragile beauty, like a butterfly with broken wings. But he was getting stronger. He would be ready soon.

She looked down at her hands, and realized that she still clutched his. She carefully turned his hands over in hers, inspecting them. Poor hands, she thought, poor ruined hands. But it would not matter. She brought them to her lips, inhaling. He smelled of light and mist and the world above. She glanced through the dome of green glass above them, toward the surface of the sea. She had little use for the many rooms of her drowned palace, but it made a good place to care for her new charge. Just then, he made a soft noise in his throat, shifting slightly under the gossamer blankets. She gently laid his hands on his chest. Somewhere in this heart was the power she sought. The mainlanders called her a sea-witch, a demon. They had stained her waters with blood and filth for centuries. For too long she had declined to act for fear of retribution from the other gods. It had been decided among them that no god could shed human blood without consequence. But now she had a vessel for her power. Now the mainlanders would pay.

She rose to leave him, one hand lingering on his hollow cheek. She hoped he slept through the night-- he did have such terrible nightmares. He looked peaceful now. She dimmed the orb of light she had cast over his bed. She never extinguished it-- the dark was too close for him—too akin to the sea's crushing gloom. With one last glance at his sleeping face, she left him. He would be ready soon. He would bring her vengeance. She walked down the empty hallway until she entered the yawning grand hall of her palace. From the endless, arched ceiling hung longship after longship. The longships were still, silent. Waiting.

Every Saint Has a Past
Aliza Dube

Sunday school, for me, was actually on a Saturday. Every Saturday morning at 9am, a perfect speed bump to the weekend. 9am was too early to be alive on the weekends. 9am was when 9 year old me wanted to be watching "Recess" on ABC's one Saturday morning. Instead I was in my pjs in the parish center staring at Mrs.Costello's kankles. Mrs. Costello was talking to us about the crucifixion. At this point in my life, I was certain that the actual crucifixion would have been less painful than listening to her talk about it.

"And Mary Magdalene was there too."

"Isn't that Jesus's Mommy?"

"No Liza."

"Than who even is this lady?"

Mrs. Costello spoke Mary's name in a careful tone, as if the syllables were made of porcelain. Mrs. Costello told us what her teachers before her had whispered about her, in that same too careful tone. The centuries had not been kind to Mary. She had the worst reputation, but the prettiest face in my illustrated children's bible. She was also the page Mama was always most likely to skip.

Papere proposed to Mamere in a church parking lot, and it wasn't his idea. A statue of Mary glared at Mamere from the churchyard.

"You fucked up." Mary's virgin lips seemed to scorn "and now you gotta deal with the consequences."

Mamere slid a palm protectively across her stomach. The baby that would be my dad kicked back. Mamere's dad sat in the front seat, his knuckles white on the steering wheel. He'd had enough of Papere's beer cans and his cigarettes and his staring. Never working. Always staring at people in cars going by, going places he would never go because ambition was something he never seemed to grasp.

"If you leave with him," Granpapere warned, "then you can never come back."

Mamere spun Papere's class ring around her too-thin fingers. She could feel the sting of Mary's gaze from across the lot.

"I'll make it work, Daddy. Even if it kills me."

Mama warned me Adam would come back for me.

"He shouldn't be texting you," she said. "Boys don't text for no good reason."

I'd protest and say that our past had been laid to rest. Dead as a doornail. He had a girlfriend now. I was smarter now. I knew I deserved better now. I silently tallied his sins against me, even made a Word document about it. When I think about him I try to see his six foot frame puking in the corner of my dorm room. I try to see his cigarette stained fingers looping around the waist of my best friend. But I don't. I see his wide brown eyes. He has eyes of the lost, of the damned. His pupils plead for the help he is too proud to ask for. Each buzz of my phone felt like the shift of a Ouija board. I didn't know how to explain to mom that you don't start playing with ghosts unless you are looking to summon the dead.

In the stories we heard, Mary Magdalene had done something bad. Us kids weren't old enough to know what that was yet. Most adults were too chicken to tell us. I asked mom once, she told me Mary had "kissed a lot of guys." I didn't understand why this was bad. Mary seemed to have it made. Mary was living the dream. But apparently not?

In the stories we heard, Mary had threadbare clothes and a threadbare face that barely had enough material left to cover the nameless sin she carried around with her. She strolled the streets of Galilee with bare feet. Her hair cascaded down her back in an act of defiance. Proper ladies didn't wear their hair like that. She was the cautionary tale that mothers of the time warned their daughters against becoming. She glared back at these crones unapologetically. She loved unapologetically. Until one day she found a love worth trading for an apology.

Daddy grew up in a trailer. Papere was always working nights, Mamere working days; the sun and the moon switching off shifts, only eclipsing for a few moments. And you know what they say about eclipses, sometimes they can mean the end of the world.

Daddy had to be real quiet during the day. If Papere woke up, there'd be hell to pay. The trailer only had one big window. Daddy would stand in front of it, trying to imagine that the trailer had wheels and that him and Mamere could roll far away from there, sometime in the night when Papere was at work. They'd roll all the way to Maine, where his grandparents lived, on the farm where there was space and not just air. Papere's yelling wouldn't reach them there. No matter how much he drank, he would never be able to get loud enough to reach them there. Mamere's thin shoulders wouldn't shake from the sound, wouldn't shake when his hand got too close to her skin. Mamere and Daddy would roll right past the little shrine of Mary in the garden and on to heaven, somewhere up North.

"Mama, let's go, let's leave while he's at work tonight." My eight year old father would beg, the hem of his mother's shirtsleeve white knuckled in his fist.

Mamere would get a far away look in her eye, her eyes always coming to rest on the Mary in the yard.

"We have to make it work, somehow." she'd say. Even if it kills us.

"What's your name again?" Adam asks, his words slurring from what I'm sure is more than alcohol. My face stings as if I've been slapped. We had become a tradition at this point, three years in a row, coming to find each other every fall. He'd found me in my new apartment, in my new room. And after all this time, he'd still pull shit like this. I blame it on the booze. I blame it on his drugs. I blame it on the fact that it's 3 am. Because sometimes, all those things are easier to swallow than the truth; that I might not mean as much to him as he does to me.

"Aliza." Stupid.

"That's good, at least I can remember your name."

I wonder whether he can even recall his own name. Or his girlfriend's.

"Does she know you're here?" I ask. He blinks back with the eyes of a child lost in a super walmart.

"I don't even know where she is," He confesses And it's one of the saddest sentences I've ever heard, even though I hate her guts. I hate her purely because she has him. He leans down to kiss me, with the thought of her still on his tongue. He tastes like cigarette butts and Jack Daniels.

"I've been drinking since Thursday." He says when he pulls away. It's Sunday now. This was something I was used to. He'd ramble off the things he'd done in the past week and I'd nod along silently, without judgement or interruption. Sometimes I'd make a word document of the things he'd told me he'd taken or drank. This way, if he ever did need to go to the emergency room, at least someone would know what to tell the doctors. At least someone would be left with the truth. "I haven't been to class in three days."

I wonder if his girlfriend listens to him like this. I pray to a God I no longer believe in all the time that she talks him down at the end of his list. I've been praying for a lot of things lately. I don't pray for her to leave him though. I love him too much for that.

Mary washed Jesus's feet with her loose, unladylike hair. She kissed each toe in turn. She promised to love him, only him. The apostles whispered about her "bad name" behind her back. She shot them glares. She had perfected and invented the "dirty look". She repented. She gave up many loves for one. This, Mrs. Costello told us, made Mary Magdalene a saint.

When Jesus was crucified, his apostles ran, they denied him, they betrayed him. Mary watched each nail sink into his skin. Mary held her love's lifeless body in her arms. She buried him. She didn't understand what all this sacrifice was for, but she stood by him to the end. Mary has sat in silence as centuries have took their turn with her, painting her as whore, prostitute and worse. Mary sought refuge in her faith, when in the end it was the thing that destroyed her. Mrs. Costello got it wrong. This, I argue, is what made Mary Magdalene a saint.

Papere threw a chair at Mamere in hospice. He was mad because she was sick of putting up with his shit, and told him so. A dying woman has nothing to lose, especially with a staff of nurses to back her. She would be dead from cancer in a week. Papere didn't want her to leave him, even if it was in death. Papere had to leave. Mamere never got the chance to.

At her funeral I got a Hawaiian Barbie to keep me quiet during the service. I got the Mary statue from Mamere's garden, too, it was supposed to keep me brave. Papere got her life insurance and all her investments. A few months later he found a girlfriend that looked alot like Mamere, especially in the way her shoulders shook when Papere was around. Daddy didn't get anything but grief.

We buried her in the churchyard under a gravestone meant for two. Mamere's dates are all filled in, all fifty years. Papere's name is there, but we're still waiting on a day. Daddy puts a bunch of Daisies next to her name every spring, for what used to be her Birthday.

"Your Mamere was a saint." Daddy tells me with the tight voice men use because they're not allowed to cry, at least not in front of their daughters. I wince. I realize a saint is not something I ever want to be.

"Can you walk me out?" Adam asks because no matter how wasted, he never spends the night. I slide on a shirt while Adam pulls his jeans on over his socks. He never takes his socks off. He'll admit that he has an issue with feet. I'll tell you that we're both just a little too afraid to be completely naked around anybody-- me with my earrings and him with his socks. I dangle the pack of Camels he left on my desk in front of his face so he remembers to take them with him. I don't need that brand of temptation under my roof.

"Of course I'll walk you out." I tell him because what else am I gonna say.

"Thanks, Liza. You're a saint," he says. I give him a dirty look, the look I reserve for people who are BS-ing me.

"Uh... I don't know about that dude," I protest. He shrugs.

"Well, you're a saint to me."

The rest of the apartment is dark. I don't dare flip on the light for fear of waking my roommates. It's too early in the morning to have to explain myself. We stub our toes and curse at every turn. He fumbles in his pocket for a light. The tiny lighter is enough to guide us to the door.

"See, smoking comes in handy sometimes," he says.

I don't argue, because it's not my responsibility to save him from himself anymore. That's supposed to be his girlfriend's job. I can't afford to be this invested anymore. I don't understand what his sacrifice is for. It's not my place to ask anymore. I fling open the front door. He pulls me in for a goodbye kiss, territory we've never trod before. And then another. And another. I forget about his girl across town. I forget that I might be letting the cat out. I forget that my roommate will kill me if the cat goes missing. I forget to fear what will happen if this cat gets let out of the bag. I think to myself, that maybe, this is all that heaven is; a proper goodbye.

But then, he is gone, stumbling down the sidewalk, back to campus, to find her. His six foot frame looks so small with the streetlights pressing down on it. I wonder how something that looks so small could have possibly fucked up my life this badly. I seek refuge in his arms even though time and time again, he is what destroys me. It will take me six months to get over this, and by that time he will be back again. Heartbreak is a stigmata for me, I wear it on my sleeve until he returns for me. I watch him until he's gone from my view and once again gone from my life. Because that's the saddest thing about saints; they can never really call anything their own.

293

An Arm Being Eaten by a Bear
Justin Barfield

I was your right hand.
The one who held all those Starbucks
cups and took down every elegantly
flowing cursive note in your boring classes and
those interviews where you squirmed around
like a worm drying up in the sun. And you let me get
eaten.
By a bear.

You're not supposed to cower and cry
like some mama's boy who never grew up;
you're supposed to stand up tall and yell
to scare off Winnie the Pooh!
And you're definitely not supposed to bring
hot dogs and chips into the woods like your
two idiot friends suggested!

Oh well. Now you can't feel the razor-white teeth
chomping through bones and breaking veins open;
at least, not now because I'm no longer attached to
you.
So I guess I'll just flop around now and
wait to become bone-filled bear scat.
Maybe it's for the best;
you were always holding me back.

Gas Station Attendant
Justin Barfield

Sitting on a gray stool on a dirty red floor
behind the cash register at the gas station,
the buzz of drink coolers, background noise,
gray pallor from the overcast skies;
the chores are all done, and all I have to do until 10
is hang out with my friends, Ezra Pound and Billy
Collins.
Then this fat, bald guy who looks like Alfred Hitchcock
comes in, I ask him how he's doing,
all he does is toss me money for gas.
Question never reached his ears;
didn't even look me in the eye.

Customers bemoaning the price of cigarettes
or about pumps not working are one thing;
being ignored like a speed limit sign? Now that hurts.

I'd like to slide across this counter,
strike this guy in his balls, kick out his
right kneecap, slam his head into the
edge of the counter, break the left side of
his jawbone, hit him in the throat with
my elbow, give his cervical vertebrae
a solid hammer blow, and finally
thrust my fingers through his eyes
and right into his optical nerves.

Instead I take his $20,
let him get his gas,
and turn to Charles Bukowski.

Making it to Cheyenne
Justin Barfield

Cheyenne ain't that far.
No farther than Idaho,
which took two days
and sleeping in my car
on a stormy Kansas highway.

Cheyenne ain't that far
to get away from the ghostly memories
of those who let you down. An open and quiet canvas
of hills and grass. A blank green slate
upon which a man can rewrite himself.

A Museum of Expiration
Jessica Henderson

I am a feather pillow,

a hunger that's never satisfied,
unborn, existing

I am an inevitable death,
insomnia, expired coupons with
uneven edges

I am what you've always wanted, you say-
dust, the inspiration from the word
"muse" that caught your attention on the page.

I am the lights you dance in,
a spirit, a being, an entity,
the intro to "The Final Countdown" before
you lose interest

I'm a sepia colored photo
Tell me about you-
a stack of free, used furniture

I am extending, the finish line
invading your personal space,
the goal.

I am three steps backwards,
lost,
camouflage

There's always an end, I think.

I am the episode of *F.R.I.E.N.D.S* you missed last week,
the story you wrote last summer,
the squeak you hear when you open your door

I am the name that you won't remember.

I had forgotten the Vastness of these Places
Jessica Henderson

Or I had forgotten you.
I had forgotten the vastness of morning.
My mind was toxic
I am defiant because defiant is
better than conformity. I had
forgotten the vastness of war. It was the only
time I forgot to be vast. I had whispers.
I had transition and I had
time. I had never returned.
I had close-a picture that looks like
someone you know.
Or someone you remember. Or someone you
forgot. I had forgotten the vastness of
our conversations. I had a word.
I had forgotten the vastness of fury.
I had you.
I had forgotten the vastness of comfort.
I know what it's like to be buried alive.

The Study of an Avalanche
Jessica Henderson

your eyes widen when you look at me
to keep from screaming

a single door left open

the weight of your words fall
harder than your bubble gum

a boy throws one shoe
with the orange laces

what if we could heat the world
with our arguments hinted with whiskey?

Ions collide every day

I wonder if the world knows
the promises we plan not to keep.

regrets are holes we all fall into

Secrets Don't Make Friends, or Maybe They Do.

B. Woods

I say, find a star for me
Then crush it.
You say no, but maybe you mean yes
Maybe you just mean maybe.
Here there is a field of grass,
Each blade sharp enough to slice.
I had a dream where a woman
With no eyes, was talking to
Someone and I couldn't hear.
The words lost on deaf ears.
So it goes, life moves on.
Its tail a plume
Of orange fire, is a curious fox
Slinking around through the trees searching
Confined by its tireless paws.
Am I the only one who can see this calm calamity
around us?
Secrets make me anxious
Or covertly happy.
Sorry that I never call or text
Anyone back.

Red Lights
B. Woods

To the waste
To the wasted ghosts downtown
To the withered hands of the old
of veterans and homeless waiting for the bus
and the sunken eyes of used-up youth:
I do not understate the seriousness of sacrifice
I search for second chances
Holding a dry cigarette between parted lips, and
exhaling lazy smoke, I think,
is this the end? I think,
is this my demise?

To become something different than you are
to become indifferent to the change

To be a fossil
crystallized in Quartz

Here's a toast to
Netflix, here's a toast to
my few friends, modern day psychiatry
sleep Zoloft coffee Wifi sex
my fresh water pearls

A CaseStudy on Feeling Exposed
B. Woods

The other day I went to the dentist

I laid down in the chair, with an open mouth

Wondering how weird it might be if I tried to ask him about the weather

Recently, and if he thought we might get any rain?

While his fingers trapped in a latex glove probed around and caressed each molar, each canine.

Did you ever think how intimate it is to show the inside of your mouth to someone else?

I think I read somewhere that teeth are the strongest bones in your body,

But I'm not sure if that's actually true.

I just know the metal contraption used to hold your mouth open is called a gag.

Once, I bought a ball-gag at an adult superstore, but never used it

And I'm not sure why I even wasted my money.

I recently learned the importance of lip liner and how much talent it takes

To perfectly trace the shape of lips and then fill them in with all of that red color.

Red like the label of that cheap Vodka we bought and took shot after shot

Red like the body of a hummingbird, which weighs less than a tiny copper penny

Red like the blood that flowed from my finger when I was a child

Flowed from my thumb like the water that was supposed to flow from the hose,

Which had a deceptively sharp silver handle.

Now I have a scar on the right joint knuckle of my thumb,

Reminding me I should always be cautious of things that aren't sharp but could be.

Like the sharpened ears of almost-friends that want to see me fail,

Claws for hands and I'm just waiting for the end of the Earth

Where success doesn't matter and everything feels

Like a strangers hand in your mouth.

What Rock Bottom Means
Sam Oppenheim

Matty said his worst morning was waking up naked in the middle of I-95 to a Maine Statie poking his ass with a nightstick. He wasn't sure what he ingested that led to his highway morning, but he knew how he got there. Oxycontin took the best of him after a terrible military accident cost him his leg. "If only I was being shot at," he said, "but a tank ran me over on the training field while I slept by a tree."

The men around the table nodded, so I did too.

He sniffed while adjusting his prosthetic and asked Jimmy to pass the saltines. His hands trembled as he ripped open the single-serving packet. There was black dirt under his fingernails. "I didn't even get to go overseas. At least that would've been an excuse for it."

"Thank you for your service, Matty," I said.

Matty stiffened and said nothing. And then: "Matt, please."

"I feel ya, Matty," Jimmy said. "Never did Oxy, though. Too expensive. But for me, it began at twenty-two when I went lookin' for my pops and finally found him with three different sharps in his pocket. He wrapped his belt around my arm and guided my hand to the vein for the first time. That's rock bottom," he said. I watched his double chin jiggle as he mimicked the gesture. His sunken eyes seemed to be swallowed by fat eyelids.

"That's not rock bottom. That's the beginning," Tommy said. His voice sounded like a cold engine trying to start. Like Tom Waits with laryngitis. "You can't go any lower than rock bottom."

305

I nodded, but the people around the table didn't, so I stopped. The conversation felt like a dance, like something I had to interpret.

There were five of us, Matty, Jimmy, Tommy, Scotty, and myself. I thought we almost looked like cowboys at a rough and tumble watering hole, our hands wrapping themselves around big mugs of beer. Instead, we wore sweat pants and drank juice. Today was my third day here and Jimmy's last. It seemed that all the y-names had known each other for at least a week.

Jimmy picked some dried food off his chins. "Well, now I'm sittin' here drinkin' my cranberry juice like it's boxed wine, so maybe this is rock bottom."

These four men weren't brothers, but they looked like they could be. They all came from hearty Aroostook County stock, built big for hours of construction and days in the fields. Their strong square heads bobbled as they listened to each others' stories. Their hands banged against the table at intervals, an anthem of fists. I felt my fingers dig themselves into my thighs.

"What about you, Caleb? What's rock bottom to you?"

They didn't know I wasn't here for drugs, but I began anyway. "I don't think there is a rock bottom," I said. "Some people hit this hard surface, and it feels like rock, but they find a way to blast farther down. But I had a shitty dad, too. So I guess we all have our reasons."

Finally, the men around the table nodded and thumped their fists. I was rewarded.

Scotty poured himself some more juice. I noticed he had already filled it up three times. "No, there's a rock bottom," he said. "I'll tell you what rock bottom is. I'm eighteen now. Eighteen. I was barely allowed in here and not the children's rehab. I started using three years ago. That's it. Just three. And one day, we went through an ounce of pot, a bottle of Captain, and started coke before we headed out for pizza. It started to snow a couple hours earlier, but we knew the roads. We were fine. Shit, we were better than fine. We were fan-fucking-tastic. But when everything started getting weird for me, I put on my seat belt. I don't know why; I just knew to. And then my friend handed me a light bulb. I didn't know what a light bulb was used for. But after I saw them hold a lighter up to it, I learned soon enough. As we drove, the snow looked like shooting stars. I felt like everything was stretching with the flakes as they whipped around our car."

"I love when that happens," I said.

"Let him finish," Tommy said.

"Thanks, Tommy. We were the only ones on the road until we we weren't. I don't remember what happened next, but I do remember finding out later that I was the only one who put on a seat belt."

"Shit."

"So that's rock bottom to you?" I said.

"No," Scotty said. "It was rock bottom when they were telling me about this and all I could think about was getting home to the stash in my bedside lamp."

***

I've learned so much since I got here. I can tell you what I've heard: that Oxycontin reacts fast for snorting and chewing, so the drug makers got wise and created Oxycodone, a pill that takes longer to kick in. I've heard that it's easier to slip a gel tablet under your tongue than a normal "chalk" tablet.

Here's what I had to learn: how lithium makes my arms hurt from all the blood draws. Seroquel puts me to sleep at a lower dose but keeps me awake for a higher one. How the definition of "dialectical behavioral therapy" applies to me. When I got here, I found out that "blue papers" aren't actually blue. But, we still call them that in Maine. I wondered if it's because we're supposed to be feeling blue. It was my third time at a place like this, but my first here. The nurses call it OL-PARK, but it's real name is Oceanlook Psychiatric and Addiction Recovery Center. I've gotten used to being checked on every 15 minutes. It made me feel like a baby. It's comforting. Now, I fell asleep with my brain calculating the differences between selective serotinin reuptake inhibitors and selective norepinephrine reuptake inhibitors.

And the outside world thought I was on vacation.

I became a walking routine. My blood was drawn once a day. My blood pressure was taken three times a day. I went to AA when the nurses weren't watching. When they were, I was transferred to my required therapy sessions to be with my own people. They asked me why I tried to kill myself. They asked me what my relationship with my father was. I began to rub my arms. I began to scratch my arms. My arms began to bleed.

And I would eat dinner and go to sleep.

* * *

"You keep your stash in your bedside lamp?" Matt asked Scotty.

"There's a hole in the bottom of the lamp, to fix the cords, so I just stuff it up there."

"I keep mine at the top of the stairs under a floor board," Jimmy said.

"Why?"

"Cause my stairs are startin' to mold so it's easy to remove a step. And so the cops don't find it." Jimmy poured himself some more cranberry juice and dabbed a saltine in it. "They barged in once expectin' a drug deal. They found me shittin' with the door wide open. Gave 'em quite a surprise!"

Scotty choked on his juice.

"Now, I know you're lying,'" Tommy said.

"Why's that?"

"Cause you're full of shit."

We were all laughing now. Except for Scotty. I felt good knowing I wasn't the outsider.

"So, what's with your pops, Caleb? 'Cause everybody already knows mine's an asshole," Jimmy said.

I felt all the eyes on me. It was my time to perform. I didn't know how to tell it, so I just did. "He took too many calls a day," I said.

"What, like he wasn't there?"

"Sure."

And that was that. The brothers went back to flexing their drug muscles. I went back to hearing how lithium cannot be ingested unless it is mixed with chlorine. And how many packages of Sudafed are necessary for creating meth.

**

It was three o'clock and Jimmy's ride was here. Because it was his last day, he had his end of care meeting with his doctors and case manager. I was sure he didn't listen to it. I watched him say goodbye to his brothers. Finally, he found me.

"Boy, you got me fuckin' scared," he said.

"Why?"

"Because I want there to be a rock bottom. I don't wanna blast through another level."

I nodded. He hugged me. My arms could barely wrap around his whole torso.

"I don't know what sorta fucked up thing takin' calls are, but I'm glad you and I get that about our dads."

I wanted to tell him that the calls came from older men. With cash. Instead, I smiled. "Thanks, Jimmy," I said.

***

He died that night. Jimmy, that is. I didn't find out until three days later, the day I got out. I was the last one of the group to go. They told me early in the morning before therapy but they didn't go into the details until my end of care meeting. Apparently, he pulled up the top step of his staircase and shot up right there. As he drifted off, he fell down and broke through the moldy steps to the concrete underneath, splintering himself as his breathing slowed to a stop.

I drove a couple hours and picked the brothers up in my car. It was strange, seeing everyone outside. They seemed all clean shaven, their clothes mostly flannel, jackets, and jeans. I didn't know what to wear to a funeral; I didn't have any black clothes except for a pair of basketball shorts. So I wore that.

All four seats were taken, but the car still felt empty.

"Yo, Caleb. Can I smoke?" Matt asked.

"Sure, Matt," I said, lowering the window.

"Matty," he said.

I smiled.

When we got there, we discovered out that no one had found the body for two whole days. I heard someone talk like that. "The body." I didn't know what to say. I just listened to this woman talk about how terrible it must have all been. To walk in on the body like that. I asked her how she knew Jimmy. Turned out she was a friend of "the father of the deceased." When she wondered why anyone would choose an open casket, I smiled and walked away.

So we stood around the body, our hands in our pockets, staring in. I don't know about the brothers, but I was unaware that Jimmy had a girlfriend. She kept kissing him, getting his makeup all over her lips, like she ate a powdered doughnut. When she moved her head away, I saw his purpled skin. I saw her left hand, a tiny ring pressed into the finger. The ring's claw was missing the diamond. "You asshole," she kept saying over and over. "You asshole, I love you."

"Well, shit," Tommy said. "I guess this could be rock bottom." We all nodded, except for Scotty.

"Does it matter?" Scotty asked. "Do we need to know?" And then: "I'm sorry."

We all decided to go to a bar and toast to Jimmy with cranberry juice. Our fists thumped against the bar with each raising of the glass. Then we toasted to rock bottom. Thump. To sobriety. Thump. To recovery. Thump. To sanity. Thump. Whatever the hell those things meant. Each drink of cranberry juice made us feel drunk, even though we weren't. And even though we weren't, we felt like brothers.

***

I dreamed about it for the next few nights. That kind of fall. I dreamed it set to music. Something classical but wavy. I dreamed it was a ballet. That heavy body, bouncing down each stair in jeté before one gave way. I didn't feel sad. Not then, anyway. I was the audience, clapping along in awe. But despite the show, I wondered how far a man could fall. I wondered if he thought to get back off the concrete under the stairs. If he could find it within himself to move his legs. Or if he just faded off, letting himself go. And then I woke up.

Contributors

Wisconsin:

Amelia Weber is a student at University of Wisconsin River Falls. Her poetry piece was inspired by the Wiccan narrative of the seasons, focusing on the turning of Winter into Spring. The thawing of the ice and the spread of vibrant, warm life to the Earth becomes an analogy for a sexual awakening.

Emily Black is a full-time student at the University of Wisconsin-River Falls, currently studying to earn a bachelor's degree in Professional and Creative Writing. She hopes to pursue a career in editing or publishing. Over the past years she's worked as an editor for her campus literary journal Prologue and as a part-time librarian, where she's surrounded by books much like the kind she hopes to write someday.

Jac Weitzel is a Junior at the University of Wisconsin-Stevens Point working on her Bachelors of Fine Arts degree with an emphasis in Graphic Design and a minor in Creative Writing. She has been published in the University of Wisconsin– Steven's Point Women's Resource Center Zine- "It's Okay To Not Be Okay" and the Riverland Community College Magazine- "The Accent". On the weekends Jac enjoys shooting photography, printmaking, and playing rugby.

Hailey Brant is a student working toward an English degree with hopes of writing novels that break stereotypes and encourage young adults to be the people they want to be. She doesn't know why she decided to go to school in Wisconsin when she hates the cold, but thinks the snow is pretty, so why not? Hailey also enjoy playing video games, drawing, and talking with people about things that don't actually matter.

Megan Geis was born and raised in Minnesota. Currently, she is attending the University of Wisconsin River Falls to pursue a bachelor's degree in English with a creative writing emphasis. She began writing when she was little and has long since dreamed of publishing her work. In her free time, she enjoys reading, listening to music, and spending time with her family.

Emily Alberti is a student at the University of Wisconsin Milwaukee. The cat life is the life for her.

Emily Talapa = sometimes eating tortellini s plain, sometimes not. A full Nalgene is always near her. She likes to write things -- first in her head and then on paper. Dream: own a St. Bernard and name it like Leo or Mrs. Norris. Currently a student at a university where she hopes to flee soon with a major in journalism, minor in Spanish and certificate in digital arts and culture. Goal: move to England where she will continue to trip on cobblestone and be happy.

Lauren Elizabeth is a 20 year old, full time student studying Arts Management and Creative Writing. Lauren spends most of her free time writing poetry and short stories on issues such as gender, sexuality, mental illness, addiction, and love. She has found a deep passion and love for writing and hopes to make it her career in the future until then she hopes at least one person is affected by her writing, "one poem at a time."

Tennessee:

Alan Rose is a sophomore at the University of Tennessee, majoring in Business Management with a minor in English. He has loved reading and writing since he was little. He probably started at least 10 books as an elementary schooler (Started as in 3 paragraphs) about anything from Star Wars related stuff to random tales of a family moving to a magical new desert area. This story is his first story that he has ever sat down, wrote to completion, and revised.

Maine:

Sam Oppenheim has been published twice before in both The Sandy River Review and The Jewish Literary Journal. He has also been longlisted at Carve. He currently lives in Maine with his dog, Baxter, and fiancée, TJ.

Taylor Mogul University of Maine Orono: Senior. Psychology Major, Anthropology minor. Bangor, Maine. Almost officially a grown-up.

Joseph Linscott is a fiction writer currently in the M.A. program at the University of Maine. Interested in fiction that moves, not necessarily with a lot of plot. Can be found on Twitter: @JosephALinscott.

Nick Bucci, a Senior at the University of Maine at Farmington. He's majoring in Creative Writing and Political Science. While striving to graduate in May of 2016, he has led the Student Senate as President and kept friends safe as Event Security Coordinator. He's an avid Civil War reenactor, Elvis Presley impersonator, and karaoke singer.

Zack Peercy is a third year student at the University of Maine at Farmington pursuing a BFA in Creative Writing. His realistic expectations are having continuous existential crises. Interpret that as you will.

Tim Bushika is a senior at the University of Maine at Farmington, studying Creative Writing. He has spent the last four years working on his craft and if all goes well he hopes to publish some of his work in the coming future.

Aliza Dube is a student at the University of Maine at Farmington.

Faith Hoatson is a student at the University of Maine. She writes poetry in the way she eats pizza: her body and mind do not know why she cannot stop, but she plows ever-onwards. She is currently toying with the idea of becoming a philosophy professor, and/or an astronaut princess.

Bethany Wicks is a freshman at the University of Maine at Farmington working towards a BFA in Creative Writing. She is braving the Maine winters for the first time because she is originally from Cheshire, CT. She loves spending her time reading, knitting, and writing.

She admires sloths for their ability to relax and sleep for long periods. One day she hopes to become a travel writer and explore the world and the animals that live in it.

Josh Carr is an English student at the University of Maine. He grew up in the small town of Calais, Maine. He has been an avid outdoors man for most of his life; hiking, camping, trapping and hunting since he was very young. He also began to write at a young age, and began writing short stories while still in middle school. Throughout his high school years he was fortunate enough to travel a little and see places people his age don't see, such as Las Vegas and the Dominican Republic. At University of Maine, he studies Professional Writing and Creative writing and is looking to start a career in video game development as well as working as a novelist on the side.

Olivia Cyr is a junior at the University of Maine at Farmington, majoring in Creative Writing, and minoring in Women and Gender Studies. She writes to break rules and expose language, even when it's difficult to put down on paper.

Arkansas:

Madison Lawson is currently studying Creative Writing at the University of Arkansas in Fayetteville with hopes to be a published author one day. She currently works for her school's newspaper, The Traveler, and is a peer editor for non-english students. She's been writing her entire life and is passionate about the subject.

Angela Blake grew up living in a series of odd colored houses in an average sized, Southeast Oklahoma town. Her writing explores this area and mixes childhood memories with glimpses of the present. She is a senior at the University of Arkansas majoring in Creative Writing. Angela currently lives in Northwest Arkansas with her husband and their five children.

Justin Barfield is a senior at the University of Arkansas. He's studying Journalism and English and can not make up his mind whether he wants to go into the news industry, or go to grad school. He grew up in Louisiana and in his spare time likes to read and play video games.

Austin Farrell is a third-year Undergraduate Creative Writing student at the University of Arkansas. he dabbles in all forms of writing, but is mainly concerned with poetry.

Minnesota:

Corey Yuman is currently enrolled at Minnesota State University Mankato. He's recently changed his major from Environmental Science to Creative Writing. He did this after realizing that Environmental Science wasn't what he truly wanted to pursue, and had loved writing for as long as he could remember. His minor is in Marketing, and he works as an assistant manager at a retail store, in addition to writing for the sports section with the MSU Reporter, and doing work reporting news and WrestlingsNewsWorld.com

Rachel Howard is a student at Minnesota State

University Mankato, she grew up living in the worlds of C.S. Lewis and Tolkien. Her imagination has always been at the forefront of her brain--whether that's a good or a bad thing, she doesn't know. Today, she is a theatre major and on-the-side writer, apparently trying as hard as I she can to get away from reality. In her writing, she tries to bring truth and tenderness into realms where dragons live, and magic into the everyday.

Arizona:

Alex Wilson is a writer, editor, graphic designer, artist, and student at Arizona State University. He's currently working on an upcoming short story and poetry collection titled This isn't a Book, it's a Cry for Help, he has done design work on promo material for THE FIFTH BEATLE, edited issues of XENOGLYPHS for OSSM Comics, and has written for Bleeding Cool Magazine. His interests include feeling conflicted about his life choices and looking at strangers until they're uncomfortable. You can find him at your nearest poetry slam, photographing local concerts, cheering on roller derby, filming artists paint, or at comic book conventions.

South Dakota:

Ellyn Julius is a nineteen year old freshman at South Dakota State University. She's an English major with minors in Spanish and Professional Writing. She is originally from Rapid City, where she has lived since birth with her mother, father and two younger brothers. She likes to do yoga, write for fun, read, watch Netflix and listen to music.

West Virginia:

Aaron Radcliff is a 20 year old sophomore at West Virginia University. He is currently studying Sports Management and Journalism with a focus in Sports Broadcasting.

Jessica Henderson is a student at Marshall University, studying Criminal Justice and Creative Writing. She was raised in West Virginia where she resides with her fiance, cat, and dog. She plans to continue her studies and learn more about writing poetry.

B. Woods is currently an undergraduate student at Marshall University, double majoring in Creative Writing and Psychology with a minor in Criminal Justice. She plans on going to graduate school to pursue her passion for creative writing in the genre creative non-fiction, but she also finds inspiration in writing prose and poetry. She lives in Huntington, West Virginia with her Miniature Schnauzer, Reginald.

Hallie Trader is a 20 year old sophomore at Marshall University, studying English Education. She plans on teaching at the high school level, and eventually finishing a master's and doctorate degree in English.

Kayla Nelson is 20 years old studying at Marshall with a major in Creative writing. Her goals are to become an author of children's and young adult fiction or screenwriter for T.V. shows or Disney movies.

Cody Huffman is a junior at Marshall University in Huntington, West Virginia. His current major is Biology, but is a soon-to-be Creative Writing major. His interest in writing was just recently sparked about a year ago. He tries to incorporate every ounce of his passion when writing.

Jess Reed is currently a Junior studying Agricultural Business and Landscape Architecture at West Virginia University.

Jordan Carter started this semester as a quasi-poet—a non-quasi fiction writer who turned her works of fiction into poetry. She has always hovered somewhere on the spectrum between a fiction writer and a poet, a "prose poet," if you will—a football player who takes ballet. Her language is deliberate, expressive, evocative, and tampers with truths—be that in prose or in poetry. But this semester, she found her footing as a poet. She moved away from keeping her ideas cloistered in sentences and rather let her lines run into murkiness, elusiveness—where the reader feels and knows, but doesn't quite know what. She relies on words to evoke images rather than sentences. She has a strong command of diction and syntax. She learned how to trim the fat and keep only that which is essential. She has brought her listeners to tears.

Kentucky:

Elizabeth Loch is an English major at Northern Kentucky University. She is a junior who spends her days writing essay for classes and writing fiction in her spare time. Her poem, Weeping Woman was inspired by the Irish Banshee myth.

California:

Joselyn Mejia is attending her third year at Cal State University of Los Angeles. She is a Business and Marketing major considering to switch to English. She has always loved reading and writing but mostly personal stories.

Martha Martinez is currently attending Cal State University of Los Angeles. She is a Hispanic 24 year old woman majoring in Child Development, Elementary Subject Matter. As a feature Elementary School teacher, she is working on creative writing.

Hawaii:

Mina Apostadiro is seventeen years old, she was born and raised on the big island of Hawai'i. She is dual enrolled through her high school's Running Start program which allows her to be both a college student and a high school student. She discovered a passion for writing at the age of seven, and has stuck with it ever since. Although she has a love-hate relationship with writing she thoroughly enjoys it. Writing gives her the opportunity to express her perspectives and ideas in a more implicit way.

Water Soup

Water Soup Press is a print and online literary journal based in Milwaukee, Wisconsin. Water Soup exclusively publishes the work of college students from around the country.

Thank you to all our contributors!

Sincerely, Water Soup

WaterSoup.Org